PERMISSION *to* PROSPER

a 'you're doing okay' kind of slumber. I am challenged, I am encouraged and honestly… I feel like Ray and God are double-dog-daring me to run a new race. Read this. Challenge your beliefs. Then do the work."

— **Carrie Wilkerson,** Author, Speaker, Business Coach

"When most people think of prosperity, financial wealth is often the first thing that comes to mind. Like Scrooge McDuck diving into a vault filled to the brim with gold and cash, many dream of riches. But real prosperity is more than financial wealth. Much more. True prosperity is a wealth of the soul. And there's no one better to walk you through this topic than Ray Edwards. Demonstrating through his own personal life and trials what it means to be wildly prosperous, this book provides a new look at a timeless roadmap for prosperity. Ray shows how you already have permission to prosper.

— **Joel Comm,** *New York Times* Bestselling Author,
Power Excavator for Financial Head Trash

"You know what's worse than burying your talents? Watching your talents go up in smoke because you're driving with foot on the gas and one foot on the brake. *Permission to Prosper* is squarely aimed at the person of faith who feels conflicted about money.

The average Christian is in a silent civil war, on one hand knowing they need to perform in work and school, yet anxious that filthy lucre will steal their heart and condemn their soul. The outcome is, most Christians are frozen. They perform quality work serving other peoples' agendas, but never get ahead and never do what's truly in their own heart to do.

Ray reasons carefully through the spiritual dimensions of money and teases out deep meaning of many troubling scriptures. "Permission to Prosper" shows how to prosper out of strength instead of weakness; how to transform work and profit into channels of service, worship and calling."

— **Perry Marshall,** Author, *80/20 Sales &*
Marketing and Evolution 2.0

"Ray is a man who walks the walk and talks the talk. He has overcome serious obstacles in life, yet created success and prosperity despite his challenges. In *Permission to Prosper* he answers a question I've often asked myself, namely "Is it OK to be wealthy, or do I need to give up everything, and I mean *everything*, to follow Jesus?" Ray supplies a much-needed answer to the question: how do we approach wealth and prosperity from a Christian perspective? If I love Jesus, does that mean I get a Rolex? Or does it mean I toil in poverty to serve the poor? Or ... is there something more, some deeper meaning for us in the word "prosperity"? Is it an invitation to live the life that Jesus promised—the life abundant? Ray's book presents a nuanced argument for the pursuit of prosperity as a spiritual practice. In a world full of charlatans and get-rich-quick schemes, Ray presents a startling premise that I find refreshing: it's impossible for anyone to prosper long-term without contributing to the prosperity of others. This book will give you a real sense of peace and purpose around the subject of money, wealth, and possessions.

— **Ben Greenfield**

"I LOVE this book. I've read plenty of content about money and prosperity and they tend to be give-it-all-away-or-you're-not-spiritual or God-loves-you-so-grab-as-much-as-you-want. Neither of those are helpful *for anyone*. In Ray's book, *Permission to Prosper,* I find a healthy, holistic view that resonates with my understanding of humanity... and a generous, loving and self-sacrificing God. Reading the pages is a breath of fresh air that liberates and empowers me to go for it and do so by helping as many people in the process, around the process and beyond the process! Thanks Ray, this will be a book I will recommend for decades to come."

— **Andy Mason**, Director of Heaven in Business at Bethel/
Redding and Author of *Finding Hope in Crazy Times*
and *God With You at Work*

"This is the healthiest perspective I've read regarding money, wealth, entrepreneurship, and how God uses those things to build his kingdom. Thanks to Ray's book, I'm better equipped now to enjoy and share the prosperity that God has generously shared with me."

— **Ryan Koral**, Founder, TELL Studios

"There are two things in my life that I strive to work toward everyday: deepening my relationship with God and living a truly abundant life. *Permission to Prosper* presents an eloquent solution to both of these aspirations. Ray shares personal stories and insights to educate the reader in a kind, informative way and it was so easy to learn and stay connected in this book. We all deserve to prosper in business and life and *Permission to Prosper* is the perfect book for the entrepreneur who is seeking to live abundantly as they go on their life's journey."

— **Paul Pruitt**

When I speak in foreign countries my first question is always, "Do you think marketing is evil?" I've never thought I had to ask that question in the U.S.—until I read Ray Edwards' Permission to Prosper. Organized religion needs a lesson in marketing for profit and Ray gives it to them in this book...with heart and logic. His premise leaves you thinking from beginning to end. Being "for profit" is not a sin...and in fact it's something to be proud of...and the scriptures back that up. I am so glad he wrote this book to dispel any notion that making money is anything but virtuous—when done the right way."

— **Brian Kurtz**, Titans Marketing and Author of
Overdeliver and *The Advertising Solution*

PERMISSION *to*
PROSPER

How to be Rich Beyond
Your Wildest Dreams

RAY EDWARDS

NEW YORK

LONDON • NASHVILLE • MELBOURNE • VANCOUVER

PERMISSION *to* PROSPER
How to be Rich Beyond Your Wildest Dreams

Published in New York, New York, by Morgan James Publishing. Morgan James is a trademark of Morgan James, LLC. www.MorganJamesPublishing.com

Unless otherwise noted, all Scripture taken from the New King James Version®. Copyright © 1982 by Thomas Nelson. Used by permission. All rights reserved.

New American Standard Bible (NASB) Copyright © 1960, 1962, 1963, 1968, 1971, 1972, 1973, 1975, 1977, 1995 by The Lockman Foundation.

The Holy Bible, English Standard Version. ESV® Permanent Text Edition® (2016). Copyright © 2001 by Crossway Bibles, a publishing ministry of Good News Publishers.

ISBN 978-1-63195-141-1 paperback
ISBN 978-1-63195-142-8 eBook
Library of Congress Control Number: 2020906405

Cover Design by:
Rachel Lopez
www.r2cdesign.com

Morgan James is a proud partner of Habitat for Humanity Peninsula and Greater Williamsburg. Partners in building since 2006.

Get involved today! Visit
www.MorganJamesBuilds.com

Table of Contents

	Acknowledgments	*xi*
	Foreword	*xiii*
Introduction	*How to Prosper in All Things*	*xvii*

Part I: Serving God: The Promise of Prosperity — **1**

Chapter 1	How I Came to Question Most of What I *Thought* the Bible Says About Money	3
Chapter 2	We Are All in Business—and Business Is Good and Moral	13
Chapter 3	Hard-Wired to Imitate God	34
Chapter 4	How the War on Prosperity Hinders the Mission of the Church	45
Chapter 5	The Perils of Prosperity	62
Chapter 6	What Is Prosperity?	71

Part II: Loving People: The Purpose of Prosperity   **83**

Chapter 7   Money Itself Has No Value   85

Chapter 8   Money Won't Make You Rich, and   91
                   Poverty Won't Make You Righteous

Chapter 9   You Don't Have to Give It Away, But You   100
                   Do Have to Give It Up

Chapter 10   How to Love People through Prosperity   105

Part III: Stewarding Wealth: The Practice of Prosperity   **111**

Chapter 11   God's Agenda for Your Money   113

Chapter 12   God: Your Wealth Consultant   117

Chapter 13   The True Secret of All Success   127

Chapter 14   How to Live this Prosperous Life   140

Chapter 15   Pathways to Prosperity   149

Chapter 16   Entrepreneurial Prosperity Plans   156

Chapter 17   The Doors of Destiny—Unlocked and   162
                   Wide Open

About the Author   *167*

Acknowledgments

I wish I could write a few pages about everyone who helped make this book a reality. My apologies to those whose name belongs on this page but isn't. No omission was intentional.

My heartfelt gratitude to:

- Lynn Edwards. Wherever we are together is home. S.O.U., my love.
- Sean Edwards, my son, and business partner. I love you, admire the man you have become, and am proud of you.
- Rob Fischer, without you this book would not exist. Your work has made every page of this book better, and I couldn't ask for a better friend or writing partner.
- Andy Mason, a friend who sticks close indeed. I am pleased to be on this journey with you.
- Robin Helton: I have been, and always will be, your friend.

The Green Room Mastermind: Mike Stelzner, Pat Flynn, Mark Mason, Cliff Ravenscraft, and Leslie Samuel.

The REI Team: You all make the work I do possible, and you make it (and me) better.

- Tami Hyatt, you've always had my back, and your loyalty is above reproach.
- Jenny Kerns, you are a never-ending source of love and joy.
- Doug Pew, your passion for writing and for music have resurrected my love of both.
- Tiffany Laughter, thanks for the years of constant care. And yes, thanks for all the laughter.
- Juan Lopez, you make us look great - literally.
- Beth Schmeisl, nothing makes a teacher's heart sing like seeing one's student exceed their teacher. Well done!
- Kris Edwards, my brother: Working with you is a dream come true. You amaze me with your creativity, and willingness to "go the extra mile".

Thanks also to: Pete Vargas, Michael Hyatt, Gail Hyatt, Mike Kim, Megan Hyatt-Miller, Brian Dixon, Joel Miller, Mary Hyatt, Carrie Wilkerson, David Hancock, Jim & Chris Howard, Jennifer Allwood, Martin Howey, Frank Kern, Ben Settle, Carrie Oberbrunner, Ed Hill, James Wedmore, Chris Ducker, Phil Mershon, Jon Acuff, Sean Cannell, Paul B. Evans, Joel Comm, Chad Allen, Jeff Walker, Jon Walker, Diane Walker, Donald & Betsy Miller, Dr. JJ Peterson, Paul & Melissa Pruett, April Sunshine, Ben Greenfield, Amy Porterfield, Stu McLaren, Chalene Johnson, Brian Kurtz, Perry Marshall, Pedro Adao, Frank Viola, Jeff Goins, Dan Miller, Chad Cannon, Armand Morin, Alex Mandossian.

To my readers, podcast listeners, clients, and customers: thank for letting me serve you, and for your constant feedback and support.

Foreword

As an author and life coach, I have seen people make dramatic strides forward as they identify meaningful and purposeful work. In addition to the sense of accomplishment and fulfillment that is released in that process, we typically see the appearance of increased finances as well. And that is where many of these same people are caught unprepared. Some produce income that is many multiples of what their parents made, creating subtle guilt or confrontation with their own upper limit challenges.

Responsible management of finances requires just as clear a plan as the business or career that created those abundant resources. Being good stewards of the wealth that explodes when we find our authentic fit in our work is not an automatic process. We must learn how to give, invest, and spend wisely. And yet I frequently see people who just assume the money will take care of itself. Or that money is just material—separate from their spiritual selves. And thus people segment their lives into those areas that are "spiritual" or "secular." The result is a fragmented life and the misuse or destruction of the wealth with which they have been entrusted. Ray addresses this artificial separation and shows the way to a more fully integrated life. Our approach to creating and managing finances certainly does reflect our values. *Permission to Prosper* presents a balanced approach to blending the spiritual and material components of our wealth.

Ray shares so many guiding stories from the Bible about how to handle our financial resources. In the story of the talents, the servants who doubled their "talents" were enthusiastically rewarded, while the one who simply maintained his little nest egg was severely reprimanded for not taking advantage of honorable methods of increase. Ray gently describes "soul prosperity" as God's method of preparing us for the gifts He wants to give us.

As may be true for many of you, I grew up in a religious framework that did not encourage "prosperity" in any form. I was raised on a dairy farm in rural Ohio. My father was a farmer and the pastor of a tiny legalistic church in our one-caution-light town, which gave me a unique perspective on the world. Fulfilling God's will meant honoring my father and mother, attending church at least three times a week, not swearing like my town buddies, and keeping my word. We scratched out a meager living by being good stewards of the farm, while silently criticizing those who went to town in search of more money. We knew the dangers of money in taking us away from the basic principles of dependence on God.

Somehow in that restricted world, when I was about 12 years old, I was able to get a copy of the little 33.3 rpm record by Earl Nightingale titled *The Strangest Secret*. On that recording I heard this gravelly voiced man say that I could be anything I wanted to be by simply changing my thinking. He talked about six words that could dramatically affect the results of my best efforts: **"We become what we think about."** I recognized if that were true, the possibilities of what I could do with my life were limitless.

While this is a biblical principle ("As a he thinks in his heart, so is he." NKJV) I knew my expectations for that phrase would not be welcomed in our house. My dad would not see that as an acceptable method for seeing and having more than what our simple farming life offered. After all, *we're just a passin' through* and wanting more opened the door to the dangers of moving away from contentment and basic godliness. I hid that little record under my mattress, bringing it out night after night to listen, dream and imagine. And I started to plan what my life could look like if in fact my thinking led the way. Any sense of being trapped began to disappear as I saw my opportunity, and responsibility, for the direction of my life.

My reading and exploration then led me to the classic book *Think and Grow Rich*. Again, I hid that message of hope for more abundance. And yet, I was drawn in as I saw the principles of author Napoleon Hill help me overcome indecision, doubt and fear, and how that confidence opened the door to increased financial opportunities all around me. And surprisingly, I also began to see how in my environment the biblical principles had been distorted to glorify poverty.

I've seen the opportunities and rewards that come from using biblical principles in business. And I've seen how business can unleash the financial abundance available for us. As Ray guides us, we can see how success in career and business is the highest compliment of imitating God. He rightly states, "Business is the answer to poverty. Business is the means by which we abolish poverty, give people dignity and increase wealth. But when we buy into the propaganda that business and prosperity are evil, we actually promote poverty and hinder God's purposes."

Helping others unleash their potential for making money is a higher form of charity than giving. Jewish philosopher and scholar Moses

Maimonides ranked various acts of charitable giving. He believed the highest form of giving was to put the recipient in business for himself, thus making him independent of charity.

Bono, of U2 fame, changed his position on giving aid to poor people. "Aid is just a stopgap," he said. "Commerce [and] entrepreneurial capitalism take more people out of poverty than aid."

Peter Greer, President and CEO of Hope International, has found that giving aid can lead to enslavement and dependency, whereas equipping people to prosper on their own allows individuals to walk into their Godly heritage.

Permission to Prosper shows us how to love people through prosperity. Benjamin Disraeli, former Prime Minister of the United Kingdom (UK) said: "The greatest good you can do for another is not just to share your riches, but to reveal to him his own." Your ability to help others discover their hidden riches is a likely indicator of your own level of prosperity.

In his engaging style (e.g., Chapter 8: "Money Won't Make You Rich, and Poverty Won't Make You Righteous"), Ray shows how to live an intentional financial life, how to *decide* to be a success, how to unlock our destiny, and then how to experience true success in multiple areas of our lives.

I commend you on doing something special for yourself and others —reading *Permission to Prosper*. **The stewardship of your time, talents, and treasure will allow you to finish well and leave a legacy that blesses future generations.**

—**Dan Miller** , Author of NYT Bestselling
48 Days to the Work You Love and *No More Mondays*

Introduction

How to Prosper in All Things

Let the Lord be magnified, who has pleasure in the prosperity of His servant.

—Psalm 35:27

Our false beliefs about money rob us of our best opportunities to serve God, to love people, and prosper beyond our wildest dreams. Our cultural programming has embedded deep within us wrong ideas about wealth, money, and the morality of business that prevent us from prospering.

Even more shocking: these wrong ideas, and not greed or avarice, are the biggest source of poverty in the world. Not only is God willing that you may prosper, He in fact desires it.

In this book, I propose three startling premises:

1. God generously offers you prosperity (this includes and goes beyond money).
2. God has a lofty purpose for this prosperity (and it's not primarily that you give it all away).
3. The practice of prosperity is chiefly a spiritual activity (and thus business and wealth creation are holy pursuits).

Tell the Truth...

If you knew it was not a sin, that it would not corrupt you... would you want to be rich? Would you like to enjoy a life in which you are not living hand-to-mouth, or paycheck-to-paycheck? In your efforts to avoid serving money, do you find yourself spending too much time worrying about money? When people say things like, "Money won't buy you happiness," do you think, "Maybe that's true, but it sure seems like it might help!"?

If so, I invite you to read this book with an open mind and an open heart. I believe that you can be rich in the fullest sense of the term. And if you are already rich, you can become even richer, and you can do so in a way that pleases God.

In fact, I think pleasing God properly in this way is one of the greatest acts of worship we can render to Him. (Read that last sentence carefully before rejecting it.)

Chances are, some reading this already feel their blood pressure rising and the hair on the back of their neck bristling. I know even from the outset, what I'm saying will be challenging to some. It might even seem heretical. There may be many questions already springing to mind:

- What about Jesus and the rich young ruler?
- What about the fact that Jesus said it's easier for a camel to pass through the eye of a needle than for a rich man to get into heaven?

• What about Jesus' crystal clear statement: "You cannot serve both God and money"?

And yet, "Let the Lord be magnified, Who has pleasure in the prosperity of His servant." –Psalm 35:27

I believe that God *does* take pleasure in our prosperity. I believe that prosperity is a gift available to every Christian, if we will simply open our eyes and ears to all that God has for us in the Scriptures.

It is my contention that you have a unique opportunity to steward wealth and to honor God while doing so. This is a great privilege, and you should not waste it.

It's Even More Shocking Than You Imagine

Some have already put this book back on the shelf, shaking their head, thinking, "Just another 'prosperity gospel' preacher!"

Others are nodding their heads in agreement with what I am saying here, thinking, "Yes, I agree with you and I want to prosper."

To both groups, I offer this challenge: what I am proposing is even more shocking and unusual than you imagine; more inflammatory; more mind-altering.

Could it be that God wants you to be *rich* and that it's part of His plan for your life? And that any deviance from this course is the work of the Enemy?

If what you're reading is making you nervous, or angry, or perhaps a bit curious, then I'm hitting the mark. I will offer scriptural truth that I believe will help you lay aside your fears and accept what God has in store for you.

If, on the other hand, you're feeling smug and secure, thinking to yourself, "I already know all this"... I have news for you. You *don't* know it. You only know part of it.

Being "rich" in the Kingdom of God means more than you may have ever imagined. Prospering is about much more than money (but make no mistake—money is included).

Rich Beyond Your Wildest Dreams

When people ask me, "Are you one of those people who promotes a 'health & wealth' gospel?" I have to suppress laughter and admit, I'm not always successful. I always want to respond, "SO, instead of the 'health & wealth' Gospel, do you prefer the 'sickness & poverty' Gospel?"

Think about it.

The word "gospel" literally means, "good news." Do you really think Jesus came to the earth to declare "the good news of sickness and poverty"?

This is obviously not what Jesus was saying.

I think God *wants* you to be rich. In fact, I think His deepest desire is for you to be rich beyond your wildest dreams. But the kind of "rich" I'm talking about is so much grander than merely your bank balance or net worth.

Some might think they're ahead of me. Perhaps they think that I'm merely speaking of "spiritual riches" and "treasures in heaven," and many of those people are (if they'll admit it) a little disappointed.

On the other hand, a few might suppose I've gone off the deep end, suggesting that a person isn't a true believer unless they're driving a Rolls Royce Ghost and sporting a Rolex Submariner on their wrist. By no means! That kind of thinking is repugnant!

To people in both camps, I would say: being "rich beyond your wildest dreams" is more than either of these two extremes… encompasses them both… and more.

How God Defines Prosperity

There is a kind of wealth that the Lord is pleased to give us that includes material wealth (money and possessions) as well as spiritual wealth (good works, holiness, and righteousness) ... and more.

How can that be possible?

What more could there be?

If all these things (money, possessions, good works, holiness, and righteousness) are included in the kind of prosperity God wants us to have, and if that is only a part of the package... what else is there?

By the time you finish reading this book, you'll know the answer to that question. Along the way, you'll learn:

- Why money won't make you rich, and being poor won't make you righteous.
- What it really means to glorify God with our wealth, and the very specific way that God is most glorified in us.
- How (and what) Satan steals from you when you fail to prosper, and why he is happy to have you "poor but spiritual."
- How the most dangerous duty God has assigned to us is also the one that's most pleasurable.
- Whether it's true that God has a specific plan for your life, a "destiny" to fulfill, and how to discover it.
- Why I maintain that business, in and of itself, is inherently good and serves God's purposes—even if the business owner doesn't tithe, never gives a dime to charity, and doesn't believe in God!

This is only a sampling of the ground we are about to cover together. I know it may seem to change everything you thought you knew about God and money. I am not asking you to accept what I am saying merely on blind faith. In fact, I am asking you to investigate the answers for yourself, and let the Scripture and God's Holy Spirit tell you whether these things are true.

I'm not asking you to make any "seed donations" to my "ministry." (I don't have a "ministry" in the way that implies, and I don't accept donations.) I am simply going to present these ideas, and show you the biblical text upon which they rest. I will do so without dabbling in subjective "Bible-trickery" and "cherry-picking" verses out of context.

All I ask right now is that you be willing to set aside your skepticism and disbelief for just a few hours—the time it takes to read this book. After that, if you want your skepticism and disbelief back, they are yours to reclaim. But I don't think you'll do that.

My prayer is that you'll understand how and why you have *Permission to Prosper,* and become rich beyond your wildest dreams. And in doing so, you will honor Christ, and one day hear those words all believers long to hear from His lips: "Well done, good and faithful servant."

Beloved, I pray that you may prosper in all things and be in health,
just as your soul prospers.
—3 **John 1:2**

Ray Edwards

Part I

SERVING GOD: THE PROMISE OF PROSPERITY

Then Isaac sowed in that land, and reaped in the same year a hundredfold; and the Lord blessed him. The man began to prosper, and continued prospering until he became very prosperous.

—Genesis 26:12-13

Far from being "the root of all evil," prosperity (including but not limited to monetary prosperity) is in fact a promise that God made from the very beginning to all His children. We need to clear the clouds of confusion, and dispel the shadowy half-truths that have been constructed around the subject of money and wealth.

The best way to do that is to shine the light of biblical truth into all those dark corners. We will see how the promises that God made to Abraham included not only our spiritual wealth and salvation, but also our financial prosperity. We will see how those promises are still valid in every way to Christians today.

"Wealth is not in making money, but in making the man while he is making money."

—John Wicker

Chapter 1

How I Came to Question Most of What I *Thought* the Bible Says About Money

• • • • • • • • ● • • • • • • • • •

The Lord was with him; he prospered wherever he went.
—2 Kings 18:7

After years of intense seeking, praying, studying, and reading the Bible, I reached a shocking conclusion. I had unknowingly accepted some very wrong ideas about money, wealth and riches. And this tragedy was compounded because I thought these ideas come from the Bible.

My understanding of what this ancient book of wisdom *actually* teaches about prosperity has allowed me to experience a more abundant life – *regardless of my net worth or bank balance.*

Allow me to explain what I mean with the following analogy:

Porn, sex-trafficking, sexual abuse, sexual perversion, orgies, adultery, fornication—these are all perversions of something that God created. Sexual intercourse is a gift of God to mankind. But He intended sex to be enjoyed within the bonds of marriage (Hebrews 13:4). However, as with other things God has given us, we quickly

3

pervert and abuse His gift of sex and make it something ugly, dirty and destructive.

Greed, avarice, extortion, blackmail, embezzlement, theft, swindling, envy, idolatry—these are all perversions of wealth, riches and prosperity, which are also gifts from God (1 Timothy 6:17). Once again, because of our propensity to abuse and pervert the good, we have invented innumerable ways to turn riches into something ugly, dirty and destructive.

Have you ever wondered why there are so many negative synonyms and terms for money and for having a surplus of it? Do any of these sound familiar?

- Filthy riches
- The Almighty dollar
- Loot
- Hard cash
- Moola
- Obscene wealth
- Ill-gotten gain

And yet... God blessed Abraham, Isaac, Jacob, Job, Joseph, David, Solomon, Hezekiah, Joseph of Arimathea, Lydia, and countless others with money, wealth and possessions. And it wasn't just a mere "side benefit"—the wealth is often cited specifically as the blessing.

Could it be that wealth, riches and prosperity are gifts from God? Is it possible we've perverted and abused these gifts? Could it be that it's their perversion and abuse that the Bible so severely warns us about, and not about prosperity itself?

What I Learned from Losing $200 Million

I just sat looking at the spreadsheet on my laptop screen.

The cursor was blinking at the end of a column, showing the total $200,000,000. Two hundred million dollars. This was the first time I had calculated all the money I had made for my clients and myself (my business is helping entrepreneurs grow their sales and profits).

My mouth was dry. The tumblers were clicking one by one in my head, unlocking a few stunning revelations.

- I was 49 years old at the time.
- I had made a *lot* of money, both for myself and my clients.
- I had managed to keep exactly zero dollars.
- In fact, I had a negative net worth. I was deep in debt.

I put my head in my hands, and felt a kind of despair I had never experienced. At 46 I had been diagnosed with Parkinson's disease. At 49 I had just realized that despite helping to create hundreds-of-millions of dollars in revenue, I was broke. Worse than broke. I owed money. Lots of it.

I had, as Dave Ramsey puts it, "Done stupid with zeroes after it."

In that moment I felt old, sick, tired—and like a total failure.

A Fork in the Road

I talked to a friend and shared part of the story with him (I was too embarrassed to tell him the whole truth). I think I was expecting sympathy or condolences. But my friend did me a much greater service for me than that. He gave me verbal slap in the face.

"Well, Mr. Edwards," he said (he always calls me that, for some reason I cannot fathom), "Now you know. The question is: what are you going to do about it?"

I said something polite (I think) and ended our conversation. He had a good point. What *was* I going to do about it?

Have you ever noticed that "iron sharpening iron" sounds like a great idea until you're the one being sharpened?

I was at a fork in the road. I had to choose if I was going to continue down the same path that had gotten me here, or finally try another way.

The heavy realization that settled on my shoulders in next moment was this: I had known better all along.

I had been handling "my" money, my way. It was time to admit it wasn't *my* money after all (clearly, because I had none of it left). I had been raised in a Christian home, and taught that we are stewards of the wealth God allows to pass through our hands.

It was time to start handling *God's* money, God's *way*. So that's what I did (which sounds so simple, but was a very messy process).

The results were startling. Eighteen months later, things were very different:

- I paid off all our consumer debts (which had been at their peak nearly $500,000).
- We had a three-month emergency fund in the bank.
- I had gotten control of my compulsive spending.
- My company grew from three people to 13, and our revenue doubled.
- I lost 60 pounds.
- Despite the Parkinson's disease, all the major indicators (blood pressure, blood sugar, cholesterol, triglycerides, etc.) showed me healthier than I had been in years!

Prospering in All Things

I was living out the Scripture written by the Apostle John, "Beloved, I pray that you may prosper in all things and be in health, just as your soul prospers." (3 John 1:2)

I was prospering in all things: relationships, business, money, marriage, and more.

I was becoming healthier, despite having a progressive, degenerative, incurable disease (we'll see about that … I remain unconvinced about the "incurable" part).

And how did this happen? I think the cornerstone of biblical prosperity is right there in 3 John 1:2. That you may prosper "just as your soul prospers." It's the one condition for godly prosperity. We can prosper and be in good health… in direct proportion to how our soul prospers.

So, what is this "soul prosperity"?

It's being *safe for success*. God wants us to have a prosperous soul to ensure that the gifts He wants to give us won't destroy us.

Forget the "Prosperity Preachers" on TV

I hope by now you can see that what I'm talking about has nothing to do with some slick-haired guy with a loud tie declaring that Jesus will give you a Rolex if you donate to his "ministry." It's not about some huckster claiming that if you will "give until it hurts" he will have God send a "magical debt cancellation" to you. That stuff is as offensive to me as it is to you.

Now, I'm not naming names, or pointing fingers (even obliquely) at any specific TV ministries. After all, it's not my place to judge someone else. But I do believe we each have been blessed with the intellect and the spiritual ability to "discern the spirits" and to distinguish between the "real" and the "perversion." In other words, most of us can watch one of these hucksters for about five seconds and we can feel the wrongness of what they're doing.

Just like the bank tellers who are trained to recognize counterfeit money by studiously focusing on the real, we want to keep going back to

God's Word to remind ourselves what true godly wealth looks like and how we properly interact with it.

·········●·········

God Sometimes Speaks Through an Ass

In the Bible, there's a story where a man name Balaam gets "the word of the Lord" straight from a talking donkey. God literally spoke to Balaam through an ass. Apparently, it was the only way God could get his attention!

A few years ago, I was talking with a friend who was dealing with terminal cancer. He told me how he was comforted by watching a certain TV preacher for whom I had little respect. Thoughtlessly, I began explaining to my friend how this "clown" made a mockery of the cross of Christ with his shameful pleas for money.

After I finished my tirade, my dying friend said quietly, "I don't know about any of that, Ray. But I do know that because of this 'clown' I accepted Jesus as my Lord and Savior, and I can face death with peace and dignity."

Immediately humbled by my friend's gentle correction, I apologized. My friend died a few weeks later. From that day forward, I have made it a practice never to bad-mouth anyone who confesses Christ.

Such an individual may be an ass. But God spoke through an ass centuries ago, and He's apparently still doing it today. For all I know, I may be an ass too.

·········●·········

Taking Back the Word "Prosperity"

Some people would like to just avoid talking about *prosperity* because of the bad connotations and trouble it stirs up. One of my early conversations with a major Christian publisher about this book illustrates the problem. The publisher said they were interested in the book, but wanted me to take out the word "prosperity." I declined their suggestion.

Look, I know the word "prosperity" is an immediate "turn-off" for many people—but I'm not ready to give up the word (or the concept). Why? Because it's one of God's favorite ways of describing His vision for our lives. For instance, did you know:

- The word *prosper* appears 48 times in the Bible
- *Prosperity* appears 26 times
- *Prosperous* appears 8 times
- *Wealth* or *wealthy* appears 43 times
- *Rich* appears 90 times, *riches* 98 times

In fact, Crown Ministries has documented over 2,300 verses in the Bible that deal with money, wealth, and possessions. So, apparently, wealth is a big deal to God. And He likes the word "prosperity." As far as I'm concerned, we're not letting the con-artists run away with this word.

The three main ways God's Word approaches prosperity are:

1. God owns everything and we are just temporary managers (stewards).
2. Prosperity is a blessing to be celebrated and even desired.
3. We must be careful to worship the Giver, and not the gift.

God's Word clearly speaks of prosperity as a blessing and He honors our prayer for prosperity both for ourselves and for others:

And Jabez called on the God of Israel saying, "Oh, that You would bless me indeed, and enlarge my territory, that Your hand would

be with me, and that You would keep me from evil, that I may not
cause pain!" So God granted him what he requested.
—1 Chronicles 4:10

But the Bible also illustrates that we can easily succumb to the
temptation to put our hope in riches instead of in God (where it belongs):

Command those who are rich in this present age not to be haughty,
nor to trust in uncertain riches but in the living God, who gives us
richly all things to enjoy.
—1 Timothy 6:17

I think God chose His words carefully, so I'm not ready to throw
out the word "prosperity" simply because it has been abused by an
unscrupulous few.

Prosperity: Better Than You Think

Prosperity is so much more than mere money. It encompasses so
much more than financial wealth. Godly prosperity is outrageously
pleasing. It's better than you or I could ever imagine.

1. Prosperity is spiritual.
2. Prosperity is health.
3. Prosperity is family.
4. Prosperity is relationships.
5. Prosperity is financial.
6. Prosperity is joy.
7. Prosperity is fulfillment.

Now to Him who is able to do exceedingly abundantly above all
that we ask or think, according to the power that works in us,

to Him be glory in the church by Christ Jesus to all generations,
forever and ever.
—Ephesians 3:20-21

Three Revolutionary Concepts that Were God's Idea

Three ideas we think of as products of modern Western Capitalist thought are in fact ancient ideas from the mind of God Himself. Those three revolutionary concepts are:

- Property
- Productivity
- Prosperity

Consider the fact that God made mankind "in His image." (Genesis 1:27) "Then God blessed them, and God said to them, 'Be fruitful and multiply; fill the earth and subdue it; have dominion over the fish of the sea, over the birds of the air, and over every living thing that moves on the earth.'" (Genesis 1:28)

It pleased God to make us like Him in many respects. As Creator, Owner and Ruler of all, God was pleased to bestow on us a measure of all those capacities and the wherewithal (property) to exercise those skills and abilities (Psalm 8:4-8).

God Says Gold Is Good

God placed the man and his wife in the Garden that He had planted "to tend it and keep it." (Genesis 2:15) Not far from that Garden was the land of Havilah, "where there is gold. And the gold of that land is good." (Genesis 2:11-12)

Many years later, when God called Abraham and made from him the nation of Israel, God gave him and his descendants the land of Israel as a possession (Genesis 12:7). God blessed them and made them fruitful. And Abraham became "exceedingly wealthy in livestock, silver and gold." (Genesis 13:2)

I hope you're getting this: that it was God's idea to make us productive (like He is) and that the result of God's blessing when we add our own productivity, would be prosperity—or owning property and goods.

Therefore, I find it odd that we struggle with the concepts of property and prosperity. For instance, many (if not most) Christians believe God wants us to live a *productive* life. Paul told the Thessalonians that if anyone wasn't willing to work, they weren't to eat. Productivity and hard work have been drilled into us as Christian values.

But prosperity and property are the natural *result* of productivity. And yet we shy away from *these* (wealth and possessions) as though they've been tainted or corrupted somehow. But as we've already seen from Scripture, property and prosperity are not sinful in and of themselves, but good—even holy. Rather, it is the evil actions of people who taint property and prosperity, when they use them for corrupt purposes.

Not only is it true that prosperity is good in and of itself—so is the vehicle that creates it: business. That's what we'll tackle in the next chapter.

Chapter 2

We Are All in Business—and Business Is Good and Moral

· · · · · · · ●· · · · · · ·

Making money is much harder if, deep down, you suspect it to be a morally reprehensible activity.

—**Rabbi Daniel Lapin**

B efore we continue a larger discussion about prosperity, let's consider where prosperity actually comes from. Prosperity originates in business.

Business is the selling of goods and services for a profit. Many (if not most) people have a deep internal belief that it is somehow evil to charge people for goods and services.

Some Christians ask: "Why not be generous, and give away your work for free? Or at least without making a profit?"

The implication is there is something morally wrong with profiting. This idea reveals a profound misunderstanding of Capitalism.

Why Charging for Your Work Is More Virtuous
Than Doing It for Free

Michael Hyatt is one of the world's most-read bloggers, a prolific podcaster, and *New York Times* Best-Selling author. He started his current business after many years as the CEO of Thomas Nelson Publishers.

By all external signs, Hyatt is successful and very comfortable with his prosperity. But that hasn't always been the case.

For the first five years of his career as a blogger, Hyatt gave away all his content for free. Eventually he developed two e-books about publishing, and began selling them from his website.

Something curious happened: even though he continued to give away his blog content for free, he was not comfortable with selling those e-books.

"For some reason, I felt like I was 'selling out,'" Hyatt says in a post on his blog.[1]

"I knew intellectually I wasn't," he says. "Nevertheless, I still felt uncomfortable."

Not only did this issue refuse to go away, it got worse.

"I would periodically get an e-mail or blog comment from someone who expressed surprise and disappointment over the fact I was monetizing my platform. They questioned my integrity and challenged my sincerity."

These stinging criticisms were uncomfortable, and felt like they were hitting a bit too close to home. But that wasn't all bad. There was a benefit to the criticism: Michael was forced to clarify, in his words, "why charging for my work is not only acceptable but *essential.*"

He cites three important reasons why it's important we charge for our work.

---

1   https://michaelhyatt.com/do-it-for-the-money.html

First, he says, it is because of "how it changes your mindset. When you start charging for your services, you go from being an amateur to being a *pro*. You are suddenly more accountable."

The second reason? Respect. Hyatt explains, "People don't respect what they get for free. There are exceptions, I'm sure, but not many. I have seen this time and time again."

Michael's third reason for charging for your work may surprise you.

"This is the most compelling reason of all to me," he says. "Charging for your services is a necessity if you are going to support your family. But even more importantly," he continues, "making money provides you with the opportunity to share with those in need. The more you make, the bigger impact you can have."

This may sound like lip-service or "do-gooderism," but for Hyatt it runs much deeper.

He explains: "I believe I have the moral obligation to make as much money as I can. Why? Because there are people in need, and I have the opportunity to help them."

Does he feel there is any danger in this philosophy?

Yes.

"If we seek it [money] as an end in itself, we can stray from our true path, and bring all kinds of grief on ourselves and our loved ones. But if we focus on doing our best work and charging for it, everyone wins."

Make no mistake, this position will lead to some harsh criticism from others. But Hyatt urges us to remain clear about our purpose.

"Making money is not something we should apologize for because of a few freeloaders who feel entitled to get stuff for free. It's not good for them. It's certainly not good for us. And it's not good for the world."

Later, we will talk about the role of charitable giving, the motivations for it, and how the role and function of giving can be misunderstood.

What If You're Not "In Business"?

Now, most people probably don't think of themselves as being in business. But I contend that this is wrong-thinking.

For example, if you work for someone else, you might think that the way you earn your paycheck has nothing to do with being an entrepreneur. You don't see yourself anything like your employer, much less the CEO of the company you work for. But while you may work for an employer, you are also actually *in* business.

Please humor me for a moment. The fact is, almost without exception, you and everyone else you know is in business. We could refer to your business as "You, Inc." You *are* a business.

You may not be incorporated as a business entity, but just like any business you offer services or goods to others in return for money. That arrangement is called "business."

The only exception to this rule might be those who work for civil service or nonprofits.

For the sake of this discussion, let's agree that you are in business. Even though you may be an employee and collect a regular paycheck, and don't think of yourself as an entrepreneur, you're still in business.

Just like any independent business, you are free at any time to go find new customers (new employers). And just like any business owner, you're free to find additional customers to the one you already have. You probably would think of this as finding a second job, or starting a part-time home-based business.

No matter what job you currently hold, or even if you're currently unemployed, it is almost certain that you have many services, skills, abilities, knowledge, and experience that could improve the lives of people around you. All of these are potential business offerings, and any time you engage with a customer (which includes your employer) you are doing business.

If we can agree that you are "in business" for yourself, regardless of your occupation, we have established a very important premise.

You see, if you have any hope of developing real prosperity, you must *recognize* that you are in business. And more importantly, you must be clear about the inherent *moral* nature of business itself.

Is Business Evil?

I propose that all of us, without exception, have been influenced to some extent by an insipid, insidious lie about the nature of business.

Here's the lie: "Business, in and of itself, is evil. Businesses only succeed to the extent that they are willing to take advantage of the public (their customers) and exploit their workers by paying them less than they are worth." (This is the lie at the root of communism.)

You may read the previous paragraph and snort, shaking your head, wondering how anyone could believe such tripe.

On the other hand, you may have read the paragraph and nodded sagely, thinking to yourself, "Yes, *of course* business is evil. *Everyone* knows that."

Most of us fall somewhere in the middle of these two polar extremes. Yet, when we read a list of words like:

- Corporation
- Prosperity
- CEO
- Banks
- Competition
- Wealth
- Investors
- Wall Street
- Profit
- Money

... we feel a vague negative moral connotation attached to those words.

This is no doubt in part because of recent business scandals. Such scandals make it much easier for people to suspect that something about business is inherently wrong.

Wayne Grudem, in his book, *Business for the Glory of God,* writes:

> *When people ask how their lives can glorify God, they aren't usually told, "Go into business." ... When someone explains to a new acquaintance, "I work in such-and-such a business," he doesn't usually hear the response, "What a great way to glorify God!"* [2]

Grudem goes on to explain that the words "glorifying God" sound like they belong in church, not in the world of business. Most of us think of "glorifying God" in terms of things the church does such as worship, evangelism, giving, moral living, and faith. These are not usually activities which we associate with business.

Grudem argues that business in and of itself is good and morally dignified. He is not merely saying that business can *contribute* to the work of the church, or that we should necessarily hold prayer meetings at the office, print Bible verses on our business cards, or take a stand against social ills. While perhaps good, these are not the *primary* means by which a business glorifies God.

Instead, Grudem shows that the following 11 aspects of business activity, in and of themselves are good, morally dignified and glorify God:[3]

---

2   Wayne Grudem, *Business for the Glory of God* (Wheaton, IL: Crossway Books, 2003), pgs. 11-12.

3   I am deeply indebted to Dr. Wayne Grudem and his analysis of business in his book, *Business for the Glory of God.*

1. Ownership
2. Productivity
3. Employment
4. Buying and selling
5. Profit
6. Money
7. Inequality of wealth
8. Competition
9. Borrowing and lending
10. Attitudes of heart
11. Effect on world poverty

It is important to understand that these fundamental components of business, the very things that many of us think of as being "evil," or at best "morally neutral," are in fact inherently good. They are all part of the creation which God pronounced "very good." These business activities enable us to demonstrate aspects of what it means to be created in God's image.

Not only is business not evil, it is also not "morally neutral." Instead, business is at its basic nature good.

As we discussed earlier, even good things can be turned to evil purposes by people with evil intent. But that does not make the things themselves evil, or even neutral.

Water and oxygen are both essential to life. I think we can agree that both are inherently good for us as human beings. But force-feed us with too much of either and they can kill us. That doesn't make water and oxygen evil or even morally neutral; they're still fundamentally good. So it is with business.

In his book, Grudem proposes that in every aspect of business there are multiple layers of opportunity to glorify God. Grudem highlights the following ways in which business glorifies God. These are ways in which business, in and of itself, is inherently and morally dignified:

Ownership

Many people think that the concept of "private property" and ownership is in itself wrong. People who hold this belief like to "imagine no possessions" (in the words of John Lennon). Even many Christians will point to the early church in the book of Acts and emphasize how those believers pooled their possessions so that no one was in need.

This one specific early church example is almost universally misunderstood. That passage is not a proof text for communism or non-ownership. Instead, it was a spontaneous and beautiful expression of their love for one another, in a gathered community, at a time of great need under a tyrannical ruler (Caesar).

God's position on ownership and property is quite clear. Private property, it turns out, was God's idea: "You shall not steal." (Exodus 20:15)

In that simple and clear commandment God established firmly the concept of personal ownership of possessions. The only reason I should not steal something from you is because it *belongs to you.* If God did not intend for us to own personal possessions, there'd be no reason for a commandment against stealing them.

Productivity

The first recorded instructions given to mankind by God were:

Be fruitful and multiply; fill the earth and subdue it; have dominion over the fish of the sea, over the birds of the air, and over every living thing that moves on the earth.

—Genesis 1:28

God designed us to be productive. He blessed us with the raw materials, the intellect, wisdom, ingenuity, and skills to invent, design, create, and manufacture goods and provide services. God loves it when we're productive, because when we're productive, we emulate God's character and glorify Him.

·········•·········

Isn't it interesting that communism, which denies the existence of God, kills productivity? Without God and without property, productivity shrivels.

·········•·········

Have you ever walked through a museum of industry, an art gallery, or even an IKEA store? We marvel at the ingenuity of the human race. We take delight in the inventions, the design, the beauty of what others have created. Not only do these creations make us smile, I suspect they also make God smile. It's like the pride we get from teaching our child some skill and watching them perfect it.

Take something as mundane as coffee. Consider how in the world all the delicious varieties, roasts, blends, and preparations have come about. Have you ever wondered who the first person was to pick a coffee bean, roast it, grind it, steep it in water and drink it? What moved them to experiment in this way with a simple bean growing on a bush? What moved them to share their discovery with others? I don't know, but God bless that person!

Productivity glorifies God.

Employment

In our drive to be productive and create new things and offer new services, many of these products and services cannot be performed by a single person alone. Building a great structure, a ship, an airplane, running a hospital, or launching a manned spacecraft requires teamwork.

God created us for relationship—relationship with Him and with other people. And it brings Him great joy to see us working together to accomplish something great. God also designed each one of us uniquely, giving us different skills, aptitudes and abilities.

We see this marvelous combination at work when God had Moses build the Tabernacle in the wilderness:

> *Then the Lord spoke to Moses, saying: "See, I have called by name Bezalel the son of Uri, the son of Hur, of the tribe of Judah. And I have filled him with the Spirit of God, in wisdom, in understanding, in knowledge, and in all manner of workmanship, to design artistic works, to work in gold, in silver, in bronze, in cutting jewels for setting, in carving wood, and to work in all manner of workmanship.*
>
> *And I, indeed I, have appointed with him Aholiab the son of Ahisamach, of the tribe of Dan; and I have put wisdom in the hearts of all the gifted artisans, that they may make all that I have commanded you: the tabernacle of meeting, the ark of the Testimony and the mercy seat that is on it, and all the furniture of the tabernacle."*
>
> **—Exodus 31:1-7**

An amazing synergy occurs on many levels when people work together. When an employer hires employees, the employer wins because they can accomplish much more than they could have on their own. They can now provide more products and services to their customers, so the customer also wins. But the employees and their families also benefit greatly from this arrangement. The whole is greater than the sum of its parts.

But hiring others or working for others glorifies God in ways beyond mere productivity. Employer/employee relationships offer many opportunities to honor God by being fair, just, kind, working hard, being conscientious and generous. God is very pleased with these character traits, because they mirror His character.

Commercial Transactions (Buying and Selling)

Stop and think for a moment what your life would be like if you could neither buy nor sell *anything*. It doesn't require much imagination to see that without the ability to buy and sell products and services, we'd all be very poor, merely living a subsistence existence.

Buying and selling are required to build wealth. If we want to help the poor, we must help them learn how to sell their own products and services, so they can buy the products and services of others.

The process of buying and selling also promotes goodwill between the seller and the buyer. When we buy something, we give the seller what he wants so we can get what we want. This fosters good relationships between people and even creates motivation to maintain healthy relations.

As Grudem points out, "We should be thankful for this process every time we buy or sell something. We can honestly see buying and selling as one means of loving our neighbor as ourself."[4]

All these characteristics represent God well and bring Him glory.

Profit

Profit occurs when we can sell a good or service for more than it cost us to produce. Profit only works, however, when the buyer wants the item or service badly enough to deem the price worth the value.

---

4   Grudem, p. 36.

As the producer of a product or service, to make a profit, we have to use the raw materials in an efficient way that is not wasteful. We also add value to a product or service because of the work we put into it.

The raw materials required to build a simple chair may only cost $25. But because of its unique design and the craftsmanship I put into building it, you may be willing to pay $500 for it. In this way, you're not only paying for the raw materials, but you're paying my "wages" for the time I spent building the chair, and for the craftsmanship and artistry required to make the chair not only useful but also beautiful.

Profit is the reward for hard work, ingenuity, and wisdom.

Jesus illustrated the principle of profit in a parable He told in Luke 19. There, a nobleman traveled to a distant land. But before leaving, he called ten of his servants and distributed to each of them the same sum of money. Then he told them, "Do business till I come."

When the nobleman returned, he called each of these ten servants to give an accounting of their business dealings. The first one came and proudly announced that he had been able to increase his investment tenfold! The master commended this servant, "Well done!" and gave him even more responsibility as reward for the profit he had made. It went likewise with the second servant who had increased his master's investment fivefold.

Finally, a servant came forward who had merely hidden his master's money in a cloth. Obviously, it had earned nothing! His master called him a wicked servant and stripped him of his responsibilities for not earning a profit.

The purpose of Jesus' parable is to teach us to put to use what God has given us. While the primary intent of the parable is to impart spiritual truth, we cannot lose sight of the fact that he does this using the principle of profit.

We glorify God when we fairly, justly, responsibly, and creatively make a profit working with what He has given us. Merely to sit on His gifts is to squander them.

Money

Money is nothing more than a mutually acceptable medium of exchange. But it is the one thing everyone is willing to exchange goods and services for. Think about it, if we didn't have money we'd all be forced into a complex barter system.

Money also gives us a means for measuring value or the worth of goods and services. Money enables commerce to take place. It's the standard by which we gauge profit. It's the currency by which we reward productivity in employment. Money makes ownership of property possible.

Often, the Bible is misquoted as saying that money is the root of all evil. Instead, it says, "For the *love* of money is *a* root of *all kind*s of evil." (1 Timothy 6:10, emphasis mine.) Money, like everything else good can be perverted. And we pervert money's purpose when we love it instead of God and people.

Money is essentially good. God ordained worship so that money (as well as other kinds of gifts) would be presented to Him as an offering. Jesus praised the widow who put her money into the temple treasury (Mark 12:41-44).

But money is not *only* good when used for "religious" purposes. Rightly understood, everything belongs to God, including money (Haggai 2:8). So, when God gives us money, we have the privilege and opportunity to glorify Him with *it in the manner in which we manage it.* When we manage money in a way that imitates His character, then we bring Him glory.

Money enables us to bless others; feed and clothe our families; engage in business; save for the future; and to *purchase goods and services for our enjoyment.* Money also gives us the opportunity to display trustworthiness, wisdom, generosity, restraint, and love.

Inequality of Possessions

I know what you're wondering: How can inequality of possessions possibly be good?

Well, let's assume for a moment there *was* equality of possessions. Jesus told a parable in Matthew 20 that illustrates what happens when possessions are distributed equally.

He tells the story of a landowner who hired workers for his vineyard. This landowner started by going out very early to find some day workers. They agreed to work for a denarius, the standard wage back then for a day's work.

But mid-morning, at noon, in the afternoon, and finally just an hour before quitting time, the landowner went out and hired additional workers. At the end of the day, his hired workers stood in line to receive their daily pay. He asked his foreman to pay those first who came to work last, all the way up to those who had worked the whole day.

To the amazement of the workers, those who had only worked an hour, received a denarius, or a full-day's pay! In fact, all the workers received a denarius, regardless of how long they had worked.

But when those who had worked the whole day also received a denarius, they began to grumble saying, "These last men have worked only one hour, and you made them equal to us who have borne the burden and the heat of the day." (Matthew 20:12)

There's more to the parable that gets to the real reason Jesus told it. But the point I'm making is that there are situations like this in which we recognize that *equal* distribution of possessions seems very unfair. We actually have to agree that inequality of possessions is most fair.

On the flipside, Jesus told another parable in Matthew 25 that clearly illustrates how appropriate the inequality of possessions is. In this parable, a business owner calls his servants to himself before going on a journey. "To one he gave five talents, to another two, and to another one, to each *according to his own ability.*" (Matthew 25:15, emphasis mine. A "talent" was a very large sum of money worth about 20 years of a day-laborer's wage.)

After a long time, the master returned home and called his servants to account. The one who had received five talents, made an additional five; the one who had received two talents, made an additional two. The master commended both of them, "'Well done, good and faithful servant; you were faithful over a few things, I will make you ruler over many things. Enter into the joy of your lord.'" (Matthew 25:21 & 23)

But when the servant who had received only one talent came, he confessed that out of fear for losing money, he had merely buried the talent and had earned nothing with it. The master called him a, "wicked and lazy servant...." (Matthew 25:26)

There are two important things to glean from this parable in terms of the inequality of possessions. First, the master distributed possessions "to each *according to his own ability.*" We don't all have the same level of skills, abilities and knowledge. Second, the reward each servant received had nothing to do with their master's fickle whim, but according to their performance. Each was rewarded "according to his own ability."

If we go to work for someone who owns a business, we don't expect to make the same amount that the business owner makes. After all, he or she has invested their own capital to get the business going. The business owner bears all the risk; the employee very little or none.

Additionally, it feels right to pay a physician more than we pay someone who washes dishes. Both are important jobs, but becoming a physician takes many years of education and practice. Also, the stakes are much higher. The physician holds a person's life in their hands while the dishwasher holds a dish in theirs.

In these ways, we see the wisdom of God in establishing the inequality of possessions.

Competition

Competition drives so many of the other aspects of business that we've discussed. Competition improves *productivity*. God gave us the desire and even drive to keep on improving what we do. We're compelled to beat our previous goals. We want to go faster, do it better, work more efficiently.

Working in an organization, or if you're in business for yourself, internally you've got your old record to beat. You want to do better today than you did yesterday. Externally, you want to surpass your competition by offering more value, better service, perhaps a cheaper product, or maybe a more expensive product but with more features and greater value.

Competition also impacts *employment* profoundly. As an employer, we seek to hire the most gifted, talented, hard-working employees. They compete with each other to get the job. In this way, competition helps people improve themselves and businesses win as well.

Competition greatly affects the *buying and selling* of goods and services. If we can produce a product more efficiently than our competition, then we can offer our product at a better price. Competition drives costs down and spreads more wealth. We see this happen all the time as new technologies emerge in the marketplace.

I remember in the 80's when personal computers began to sell. They were very expensive and nowhere near as powerful or versatile as they are today. Through competition the prices have *dropped,* making them much more affordable to nearly anyone.

Of course, competition greatly impacts *profits*. Business owners are always trying to produce their products and services more efficiently, or they seek to offer options that make their goods and services more competitive. In this way, they can increase their profits and the consumer wins too. What this kind of competition does is produce better goods and services at "competitive" prices. Competition drives costs down *and spreads more wealth.*

It's easy to see how good, clean competition glorifies God. In competition, we exercise our God-given drive to excel. We seek to create new things. We strive to do better than we have in the past. We may benchmark our competition, but only to surpass them.

The Apostle Paul urges us, "Finally then, brethren, we urge and exhort in the Lord Jesus that you should abound more and more, just as you received from us how you ought to walk and to please God." (1 Thessalonians 4:1) Surely this doesn't only apply to spiritual things, but to all we do.

We see then, that through competition everyone wins. Businesses earn more profit, employees improve themselves, and consumers get more and better products and services at competitive prices.

Do you not know that those who run in a race all run, but one receives the prize? Run in such a way that you may obtain it.
—1 Corinthians 9:24

Borrowing and Lending

The Bible has a lot to say about the abuses of borrowing and lending, but does not condemn these practices. As a matter of fact, we've already looked at the parable Jesus told about the servants who were entrusted with varying amounts of funds to invest. Those who invested well (loaned their master's money to others) and made a profit were commended.

And of course, if loaning money to others is permitted and even encouraged in the Bible, then borrowing is as well. You can't loan money if there's no one to borrow it.

Once again, we see the tight connection between borrowing and lending and some of the other elements of business we've discussed like: ownership, commercial transactions, profit, money, and the inequality of possessions.

Borrowing and lending can please God because we're exercising our God-given resources and ingenuity to "be fruitful and subdue the earth." For instance, if we have the wherewithal to loan money to others, we help them achieve things they could not achieve without our loan. And by helping them, they help us earn interest on money that would've otherwise "just sat there." We send our dollars out like little envoys creating good!

By borrowing money, we can start a business and build something with greater potential than without the loan.

Wayne Grudem provides a beautiful example of the power of borrowing and lending. When we travel to another city and rent a car or rent a hotel room, by means of borrowing that car or hotel room, we increase our prosperity. It's as though we owned a car or room in any city we wish to visit.

Grudem writes, "In this way, the process of borrowing and lending multiplies the available wealth in the world more times than it is possible to calculate. If we could not borrow and lend money, but had to operate only on a cash basis, the world would have a vastly lower standard of living."[5]

Thus, borrowing and lending glorify God and enable us to accomplish and enjoy much more than without them.

Attitudes of Heart

Keep your heart with all diligence, for out of it spring the issues of life.

—Proverbs 4:23

---

5   Grudem, pp. 71 and 73.

Neither God, nor any parent, nor an employer, nor a customer, nor anyone else is ever satisfied with heartless performance. Mere activity without heart is a sham. And it's equally true that activity combined with wrong motivations perverts our activities, making them something ugly.

And whatever you do, do it heartily, as to the Lord and not to men, knowing that from the Lord you will receive the reward of the inheritance; for you serve the Lord Christ.
—Colossians 3:23-24

Attitudes of heart make the difference between practicing the above elements of business in a God-honoring way, or abusing and distorting them for our own gain and others' loss. Instead, our heart attitudes should exude love and appreciation for God and others. We should exercise humility being joyful and thankful for what God and others have provided for us.

We should treat others with respect and dignity, looking for ways to improve their lot as we improve ours. We seek to conduct business and compete in the marketplace fairly, honestly and righteously.

And as our wealth and possessions increase, we must remember that these all come from God. We must never worship them, but only Him who gave them to us. We must be generous, looking to imitate God and bless others through what He has given us.

In all these elements of business, we see that they are in fact tests of the purity of our hearts. This also serves as a sober warning that any of these elements of business can be perverted, spoiled and misappropriated. But the fact that many dishonest people misuse and abuse business is no reason to abandon it or view it as something evil or even morally neutral. Business, rightly practiced, truly brings glory to God and benefits people.

Effect on World Poverty

Grudem encourages us to "*rejoice* in the God-given *goodness of business in itself* pursued in obedience to God."[6] He urges us to "*enjoy* and thank God for: ownership, productivity, employment, commercial transactions, profit, money, inequality of possessions, competition, and borrowing and lending."[7]

And we should gladly engage in all those business activities always keeping the poor in mind and seeking ways to ease their situation. Grudem believes, and I agree with him, "*the only long-term solution to world poverty is business.*"[8] The reason for this is that business provides products and services and produces jobs. Jobs and the availability of products and services produce wealth. Without jobs and the availability of products and services there is no prosperity.

I'm aware of a beautiful example of this taking place in Ethiopia today. Sixteen years ago, a particular group of people in Ethiopia were extremely poor. They were coffee growers, but due to poor agricultural practices, lack of a market for selling their coffee, and strict government regulations, they were kept poor.

But a church in northern Idaho sent some businessmen to Ethiopia to work with these people. They taught them how to get the most from their crops and give back to the soil. These businessmen then worked with the government and established an export business. Where the coffee growers used to get only pennies on the dollar, they now enjoy significant profits. Their coffee arrives in the U.S. today by the container-full! Business has transformed these people from poverty to prosperity.[9]

Wherever poverty exists there will always be barriers and challenges to creating new businesses. But those are the kinds of challenges that entrepreneurs love to sink their teeth into.

---

6   Grudem, p. 79.
7   Grudem, pp. 79-80.
8   Grudem, p. 80.
9   http://www.dominiontradingcoffee.com/about.php

One such entrepreneurial enterprise, Kiva.org, facilitates unique opportunities for both lenders and borrowers. In this way, nearly anyone can offer a microloan to help the poor launch new businesses. As of the writing of this book, Kiva has brokered nearly $1 billion in microloans since its founding in 2005! About 2.4 million loan recipients in 83 countries have benefited from these loans.[10]

What you're reading here is one of the reasons I've shifted my business from one that directly provides clients with copywriting services to one that helps and trains others to succeed in business. I find great joy in helping others build their businesses and prosper. My hope is that as they prosper they will help other entrepreneurs as well.

This is why I believe that business, complete with all its many facets, is good and brings glory to God.

---

10   https://www.kiva.org/about

Chapter 3

Hard-Wired to Imitate God

· · · · · · · · ●· · · · · · · · ·

God created us so that we would imitate Him and so that He could look at us and see something of His wonderful attributes reflected in us.

—Wayne Grudem

Why do we work? I realize you are probably thinking, "to get paid." That is most certainly part of the answer—it is usually the first motivation.

But there has to be a bigger reason to work than *just* getting paid. Our lives diminish when we are not engaged in some kind of productive activity. The stories of people who are hale and hearty right up to their retirement, then die less than a year later, are so common that they have almost become proverbial. Work seems to provide such significant meaning in a person's life that without it we lose life purpose. Without work, we die.

So why are humans driven to work, to create things, to invent things, and do all the other productive activities we do during any given day?

The answer: we are imitating God. We can't help it. God is *the Creator, the Builder, the Inventor* and *the Entrepreneur.* Even those who don't believe in God imitate Him unwittingly. Oh, they may come up with other reasons for their good behavior, such as fulfilling "their social contract," but the fact is they are imitating their Creator.

God *created* us so that we would imitate Him. It's in the Bible:

> *So God created man in His own image; in the image of God He created him; male and female He created them.*
> **—Genesis 1:27**

The implications of this concept are astonishing. Why would God create us in His image? To do so means we are like God in some very important ways. We represent God on the earth. As Wayne Grudem puts it: "This means that God created us to be more like Him than anything else He made."[11]

And immediately after creating Adam and Eve (humans), the Bible comments, "Then God saw everything that He had made, and indeed it was a very good." (Genesis 1:31) He looked at us and was very pleased!

This idea of imitating God, of representing His character and nature, is echoed by the apostle Paul who says, "Therefore be imitators of God as dear children." (Ephesians 5:1) God, our Father, is the Creator. He is the ultimate optimist. The quintessential entrepreneur. And we are meant to imitate Him.

Genesis 2:2 offers an additional powerful example of our imitation of God. There it says:

> *And on the seventh day God ended His work which He had done, and He rested on the seventh day from all His work which He had*

---

11 Grudem, p. 14.

done. Then God blessed the seventh day and sanctified it, because in it He rested from all His work which God had created and made.

When God set apart the seventh day as a day of rest, He did so not because He was tired, but because He was setting an example for us to follow. We discover this later in the story, when God gives Israel the Ten Commandments. The fourth commandment is to "keep the Sabbath (or seventh day) holy" as a day of rest. The argument God provides for establishing this law is His own example (Exodus 20:8-11). He wants us to mimic Him.

The reason I bring this up here isn't because I wanted to write about resting, or taking a Sabbath rest (though I think we should). But notice that as humans we are so *driven to work*, so hard-wired to imitate God when it comes to work, that God literally had to tell us to STOP! Take a break! Rest from your work one day a week.

In addition to imitating God, there's something else very significant that we learn about who we are with respect to work. When God created the first man and woman, He told them:

Be fruitful and multiply; fill the earth and subdue it; have dominion over the fish of the sea, over the birds of the air, and over every living thing that moves on the earth.
—Genesis 1:28

Then, a little later we read, "Then the Lord God took the man and put him in the garden of Eden to tend and keep it." (Genesis 2:15) And Psalm 8:6 adds, "You have made him [mankind] to have dominion over the works of Your hands; You have put all things under his feet."

We see from these passages that God not only hard-wired us to work *like* Him, but to work *with* Him. He delegated work to us: to rule over the earth, subdue it (master it), manage it, and take care of it. This is a daunting but noble purpose. Long before there was any kind of "ministry" to engage in, God gave us work. This demonstrates how very holy and God-ordained work is.

God Is an Entrepreneur, and So Are You

Jean-Baptiste Say, the French economist who first coined the word *entrepreneur*, explained, "The entrepreneur shifts economic resources out of an area of lower and into an area of higher productivity and greater yield."

God, of course, is the original, the consummate Entrepreneur. He created the world from nothing and then took the raw materials He had created and "shifted those resources out of an area of lower and into an area of higher productivity and greater yield." With those raw materials He made mountains, rivers, oceans, and all manner of living things.

Being made in His image, we all imitate Him creatively in some way. We all carry the DNA of *the* Entrepreneur, with a capital "E." And this "shifting of economic resources out of an area of lower and into an area of higher productivity" is what God created us to do. He created us all with some measure of entrepreneurial spirit.

As those made in His image, we're constantly seeking to improve things. We're incessantly inventive. We can't help ourselves! Whether it's an administrative assistant designing a sleeker spreadsheet; a mechanic coming up with a better way to change brakes on a car; a mom devising a clever way to get her kids to do chores; or a person launching a new business—these are all examples of the entrepreneurial spirit we all possess.

And if we're willing to accept Jean-Baptiste Say's definition of *entrepreneur*, then we recognize that the end product of our entrepreneurial efforts is "higher productivity and greater yield." And the natural result of higher productivity and greater yield is prosperity. In other words, when we imitate God and exercise our God-given abilities as entrepreneurs, we will prosper. It's like a mathematical equation: x + y = z.

I'm not saying that everything we try will succeed. What I am saying is that the natural, expected outcome of entrepreneurial enterprise is prosperity.

Co-Laboring with God

Collaboration means "to work together" or "co-labor." Many Christians are familiar with the idea that we "co-labor" with God. Often, we tend to think of co-laboring with God as something that is limited to ministry or spiritual endeavors. But we find many examples in Scripture where God was intimately involved in the *business* affairs of people. Here are just a few such examples:

> *Then Isaac sowed in that land, and reaped in the same year a hundredfold; and the Lord blessed him. The man began to prosper, and continued prospering until he became very prosperous.*
> **—Genesis 26:12-13**

> *The Lord was with Joseph, and he was a successful man; and he was in the house of his master the Egyptian. And his master saw that the Lord was with him and that the Lord made all he did to prosper in his hand. So Joseph found favor in his sight, and served him. Then he made him overseer of his house, and all that he had he put under his authority. So it was, from the time that he had made him overseer of his house and all that he had, that the Lord blessed the Egyptian's house for Joseph's sake; and the blessing of the Lord was on all that he had in the house and in the field.*
> **—Genesis 39:2-5**

He causes the grass to grow for the cattle, and vegetation for the service of man, that he may bring forth food from the earth, and wine that makes glad the heart of man, oil to make his face shine, and bread which strengthens man's heart.
—Psalm 104:14-15

In the above examples, God was intimately involved in Isaac's and Joseph's lives and in their work. The Psalms example shows how God is generally involved in all our work.

We need to change our perspective and recognize God's sovereign and gracious hand in all we do and accomplish. We must recognize that God is an active Agent in all our work. Additionally, I believe we need to deliberately *include* Him in all our business efforts.

By "include Him" I mean something more than having a quick "token prayer" at our staff meetings, or printing Bible references on our business cards, or putting a fish sticker in our store window. So, what do I mean exactly?

There's a remarkable phrase contained in Colossians 2:3. There, Paul says, in Christ "are hidden all the treasures of wisdom and knowledge." That's ALL the treasures of wisdom and knowledge. That excludes nothing. Therefore, including God in your business and work means, in part, tapping directly into those "treasures of wisdom and knowledge."

What's your biggest challenge in your work right now? What's that hurdle that has you stumped? What's the one problem that you know if you solved it would expand your business like nothing else? Jesus possesses the wisdom and knowledge to solve it, and His help is there for the asking.

Jesus wants to be involved in all aspects of our life—especially business. How can I claim that? Because we spend more of our waking hours and more of our energy conducting business (working) than anything else.

> *And whatever you do, do it heartily, as to the Lord and not to men, knowing that from the Lord you will receive the reward of the inheritance; for you serve the Lord Christ.*
> **—Colossians 3:23-24**

Now some reading this might argue, "Why would Almighty God be concerned about my petty work issues?" This kind of "little old me" attitude may sound pious to some. Such statements have a pseudo-humble ring to them, but check this out:

> *Therefore humble yourselves under the mighty hand of God, that He may exalt you in due time, casting all your care upon Him, for He cares for you.*
> **—1 Peter 5:6-7**

If you read that passage closely, Peter tells us what humility before God looks like. We humble ourselves before God by "casting all our care upon Him, for He cares for us." We're not pestering Him or boring Him with our issues. On the contrary, we demonstrate humility toward God when we acknowledge that He cares about us so much that He wants to be involved in all our business dealings and issues.

Abraham

Abraham is a very special example of someone who experienced God's blessing and involvement in his work. As a result, Genesis 13:2 simply declares, "Abram was very rich in livestock, in silver, and in gold."

God chose Abraham to be the conduit through which the world would be blessed.

It's remarkable that God singled out Abram (his name before God changed it to Abraham) from his relatives. You see, Abram was an idol worshiper before he met God. But God sought him out. We read God's call on Abram's life in Genesis 12:1-3:

Now the Lord had said to Abram: "Get out of your country, from your family and from your father's house, to a land that I will show you. I will make you a great nation; I will bless you and make your name great; and you shall be a blessing. I will bless those who bless you, and I will curse him who curses you; and in you all the families of the earth shall be blessed."

Paul summarizes God's covenant promise to Abraham succinctly in Romans 4:13. With insight from the Holy Spirit, Paul interprets God's promise to Abraham and his offspring explaining that they would be "heirs of the world."

For the promise that he would be the heir of the world was not to Abraham or to his seed through the law, but through the righteousness of faith.
—Romans 4:13

This is a remarkable statement indicating that God's promise to Abraham extended far beyond the tiny acreage of Israel and beyond Abraham's son Isaac and his descendants. Also, the fact that God's promise came "through the righteousness of faith," is monumental. Why? Because faith renders God's promise to Abraham binding on us who are in Christ. In other words, you and I are "heirs of the world."

If we have placed our faith in Christ, we are heirs of the world first because we are Abraham's children. Abraham is the "father of all those who believe." (Romans 4:11) Paul goes on to explain:

Therefore it is of faith that it might be according to grace, so that the promise might be sure to all the seed, not only to those who are of the law, but also to those who are of the faith of Abraham, who is the father of us all.

—Romans 4:16

But even more importantly, we are heirs of the world because we are in Christ. Since Christ is heir of the world, in Him God has made us heirs with Him.

God, who at various times and in various ways spoke in time past to the fathers by the prophets, has in these last days spoken to us by His Son, whom He has appointed heir of all things, through whom also He made the worlds.

—Hebrews 1:1-2

The Spirit Himself bears witness with our spirit that we are children of God, and if children, then heirs—heirs of God and joint heirs with Christ, if indeed we suffer with Him, that we may also be glorified together.

—Romans 8:16-17

He who did not spare His own Son, but delivered Him up for us all, how shall He not with Him also freely give us all things?

—Romans 8:32

Paul summarizes both points in Galatians 3:29 when he says, "And if you are Christ's, then you are Abraham's seed, and heirs according to the promise." And in Christ, "You were sealed with the Holy Spirit of promise, who is the guarantee of our inheritance until the redemption of the purchased possession, to the praise of His glory." (Ephesians 1:13-14)

Ponder the magnitude of what we've been uncovered in these last few pages:

- By faith in Christ, we have become Abraham's children.
- As Abraham's children, we too are heirs of the promise God made to him.
- God's promise is that Abraham would be "heir of the world."
- Both as Abraham's children, and more importantly, as God's children in Christ, we are heirs of the world.
- God has sealed His promise to us by giving us His Holy Spirit.

What Does It Mean to Be Heirs of the World?

The fact that we are heirs of the world in Christ should astonish you. If it doesn't, I propose you haven't fully understood it. If we are heirs of the world, and recipients of the promise made to Abraham, we should look at what Abraham received: material wealth (gold, silver, and livestock), a thriving business, favorable outcomes in his dealings engineered by God, and restored physical vitality in his old age (Abraham was 100 when his son Isaac was born to Abraham's wife Sarah—who was 91).

Most amazing of all, it was through Abraham's lineage God would bring forth Jesus the Messiah. Part of the inheritance is the redemption of Creation through Jesus!

Comprehending the scope of "the promise" of "the inheritance" should fundamentally alter our perspective on everything, including:

1. **Perspective on wealth.** You are an heir of the world, a promise that God has sealed by giving you Himself in the form of the Holy Spirit. So regardless of your current financial situation, you are wealthy beyond measure. The wealth of a Warren Buffett or Bill Gates doesn't even move the needle by comparison. And you must remember that the inheritance is not only spiritual, but

also material: Abraham was rich in gold and silver and livestock (business/work). This too is a rightful part of your inheritance.

2. **Perspective on ownership.** We are co-heirs with Christ and with each other. We didn't just win the "Greatest Powerball Ever" so that we could squander away our winnings (like most lottery winners do). We have been entrusted as co-heirs of a fortune so vast, so colossal, so mind-boggling that our only logical recourse is to manage it wisely, as His Regents (representatives of the King), and to rely on Him to help us manage it.

3. **Perspective on joy and achievement.** Because we are heirs of the world, we do not have to achieve so that we can experience joy; *we have the power to joyously achieve.* There is *no* failure— unless we merely give up. If we are drawing breath we can stand back up after every fall, having learned something in the process. Like King David said so many years ago, "Because the Lord is my Shepherd, I lack nothing." (author's paraphrase)

4. **Perspective on life.** As God's kids and heirs of the world, we should be the most joyful, loving, generous, optimistic people on earth! We are the most prosperous people in every sense of the term.

5. **Perspective on trials.** Hardships of any and every kind, financial setbacks, health problems, or persecution should not phase us. No matter how extreme the trial, it's barely a blip on the screen of eternity and has no bearing whatsoever on our inheritance. Christ's inheritance is crash-proof.

   a. We are truly hardwired to imitate God! And imitating Him will have a profound impact on how we conduct ourselves in this life and with those around us. We are co-heirs of the world: we are princes, yet we so often behave like paupers.

Chapter 4

How the War on Prosperity Hinders the Mission of the Church

· · · · · · · ●· · · · · · · ·

"Seek not proud riches, but such as thou may just get justly, use something, distribute cheerfully, and leave contentedly."
—Sir Francis Bacon, 1625

I believe there is a war on prosperity being fought on several fronts, and that this war hinders the church's mission to go and make disciples of all nations (Matthew 28:18-20). I'm not saying that lack of funds is the greatest, or even a significant deterrent to world evangelization. After all, God owns it all. As one missiologist put it, "God's work, in God's way, never lacks God's supply."

Instead, I'm saying that fundamentally, *the way in which we conduct business is crucial to the spreading of the Gospel.*

Paul alludes to the high value he placed on business in both his letters to the Thessalonians. In 1 Thessalonians 2:9, he wrote, "For you remember, brethren, our labor and toil; for laboring night and day, that we might not be a burden to any of you, we preached to you the gospel of God."

Paul is not referring to "laboring in the Gospel" here. He's saying that he, Silas and Timothy *labored in their businesses*—working overtime—in order not to burden the Thessalonians financially *and* to give them a godly example of what it means to follow Jesus in business. Paul and his companions' conduct in business *gave credence to the Gospel* and *provided a real-life example* for the Thessalonians to follow. That's discipleship!

In 2 Thessalonians 3:7-9 Paul reminded them again:

> *For you yourselves know how you ought to follow us, for we were not disorderly among you; nor did we eat anyone's bread free of charge, but worked with labor and toil night and day, that we might not be a burden to any of you, not because we do not have authority, but to make ourselves an example of how you should follow us.*

The way that Paul and his co-workers conducted themselves in business was a vital element of the Gospel, showing the Thessalonians what it looks like to follow Jesus in everyday life.

Finally, in 1 Thessalonians 4:11, Paul urged them, "Aspire to lead a quiet life, to mind your own business, and to work with your own hands, as we commanded you." It's clear that in the very short time that Paul and his companions preached the Gospel to the Thessalonians, their message also focused on the important topic of business. Both in their teaching and by their example, Paul and his companions demonstrated the key role that business plays in the spread of the Gospel. How these new followers of Christ conducted business was a key aspect of their walk in Christ.

Let's look at some additional reasons why business holds such an important role in accompanying the message of the Gospel. By conducting business in a godly manner:

- We're doing the will of God by serving the Lord, not men. (Ephesians 6:5-9)
- We're imitating Christ. (Colossians 4:1)
- We maintain a good reputation with outsiders. (1 Timothy 3:7-8)
- We prevent the name of God and His doctrine from being blasphemed. (1 Timothy 6:1-2)
- We make the Gospel attractive to unbelievers. (Titus 2:9-10)
- We maintain a good conscience and are commended before God. (1 Peter 2:18-20)

Think about it—most of us spend more of our lives working than doing anything else. By what means other than work can we gain a good reputation with unbelievers? What better way to demonstrate to the world the power of Christ to change a life than through our work and business dealings!

Or, by contrast, what better way to damage the cause of Christ and soil the Gospel than through shady business dealings, greed, dishonesty, slackness, and waste?

It is therefore my belief that when business and the prosperity that naturally flows from it are undermined, so is the Gospel. It's clear from the Scriptures that business is one of the pivotal areas of our lives that needs transforming. So, a well-run business and its attending prosperity offer the world a clear witness of the transformation Christ brings about in people.

But as with any war, the war on prosperity is fought on many fronts, with a variety of weapons, strategies, tactics and propaganda.

We don't want to give the devil too much credit. Jesus warned us that the devil comes to steal, kill, and destroy (John 10:10). We know from the account of Job, Jacob and others in the Scriptures that the devil sometimes directly attacks the prosperity of the righteous. Satan's attacks are also clearly meant to have a profound impact on the subject's relationship with God and influence in the world.

The devil may also hinder Kingdom work by subtly and deceitfully convincing us that prosperity is something evil. We can always assume that the devil will seek to pervert anything God has designed and declared to be good. This applies to relationships, sex, religion, politics, business, money and countless other things.

God created wealth and has given us a wonderful array of possessions and gifts to enjoy. But Satan has perverted, counterfeited, and polluted so many of these things. Many of Satan's ploys negatively impact our views on prosperity. The devil knows that if he can get us to call "bad" what God has declared "good," he can undermine the work of God.

In the case of prosperity, the devil has often twisted it to become something dirty and dishonest, instead of something with which we can honor and glorify God.

Fortunately, the deceiver's ploys are not always successful. Consider the following example. When writing the Corinthian church about a collection for the Lord's people in Jerusalem, Paul boasted about the Macedonian churches:

> *Moreover, brethren, we make known to you the grace of God bestowed on the churches of Macedonia: that in a great trial of affliction the abundance of their joy and their deep poverty abounded in the riches of their liberality.*
> **—2 Corinthians 8:1-2**

This is remarkable! In spite of Satan's attacks on these churches through severe trials and poverty, God's grace shown through powerfully. Even though the Macedonian churches were impoverished themselves, the abundant joy they reaped from God's grace bubbled up into *rich generosity!* This is something only God can do, but wants to do in us and through us.

The war on prosperity says, "You're impoverished *yourself. You* have nothing to give." This thinking stifles our growth as individuals and as a church. It limits our work for God's Kingdom to the puny contributions we make apart from His grace.

But in faith coupled with God's grace, even the two small copper coins of the widow swell to more than all that the wealthy put into the temple treasury (Mark 12:41-44). The one giver says, "Look at me. Look at what I'm giving!" The other says, "Look at God. Stand in awe of what only He can do!" And in this way, we become channels of His grace and of His wealth.

Now may He who supplies seed to the sower, and bread for food, supply and multiply the seed you have sown and increase the fruits of your righteousness, while you are enriched in everything for all liberality, which causes thanksgiving through us to God.
–2 Corinthians 9:10-11

Whatever Satan throws at us, God's grace is infinitely bigger. This applies to our finances as an individual, as a family, as a business, and as a church.

The War on the Wealthy

"It's like there's a suspicion that we must have done something underhanded to get our wealth."
—Doug Seebeck

The war on prosperity not only attacks those with little means but also the wealthy. We might call this battle the "slaughter of success." The call for the "one percent" to divide their wealth and "give back" to "the ninety-nine."

Now you might equate this line of thinking purely as political, but I assure you that it's alive and well in the church as well. I believe that this is one of the devil's most devious propaganda campaigns in which he tries to put a self-righteous twist on coveting what the wealthy have.

Wealth *cannot* be redistributed equally. It only results in even more inequality and division. This kind of thinking is communism. It's Marxism. Communism has never worked in any country, at any time in history, under any circumstances. What communism has demonstrated is that it places the wealth and power in the hands of an elite few (the government) and suppresses the masses—the very thing it purports to undermine.

Some entertain the false notion that the early church in Acts practiced a form of communism when Christians sold their property and distributed the money so that no one lacked. But the big difference between what the early church was doing and communism is that those Christians *voluntarily* shared their goods and money out of love for each other. It also appears to have been done in a special instance due to persecution.

Just as the Pharisees looked down on the poor of their day, many in the church look down on the wealthy today. I believe this is largely due to a misunderstanding of what Jesus and Paul said about the rich and wealth.

When we penalize the wealthy for being wealthy, we unwittingly kill productivity, competition, continuous improvement, generosity, and a host of other godly values among the wealthy. If we were to somehow redistribute wealth, wouldn't the wealthy cry out, "Why should I bust my butt, only to have my profits taken away?"

At the same time, the so-called redistribution of wealth feeds a sense of entitlement among those "less fortunate." As a result, we kill their work drive and its attending values as well. "Why should I bust my butt, when someone is willing to hand me what I need and want?"

Doug Seebeck, with Partners Worldwide, has observed that decades of handouts in developing countries have created a "spirit of passivity" among the recipients. Building businesses, not handouts, restores an economy and the dignity and integrity of its people.[12]

Business is the answer to poverty. *Business is the means by which we abolish poverty, give people dignity and increase wealth.* But when we buy into the propaganda that business and prosperity are evil, we actually promote poverty and hinder God's purposes.

God's counsel to the prosperous is that they "Do good, that they be rich in good works, ready to give, willing to share, storing up for themselves a good foundation for the time to come." (1 Timothy 6:18-19) But when the wealthy are attacked or ostracized for being wealthy, we lose them: their gifts, talents and resources, thus hindering the mission of the church.

Is Money Evil?

Another propaganda message hurled against prosperity is that money is evil. Where does the idea of money being evil come from? Not from the Bible. It has its roots in the philosophy of Plato, which permeated the Church in the form an early heresy known as Gnosticism. Gnosticism taught that the physical world was evil, and only the "spiritual world" could be good. In fact, it's this very heresy that the Apostle John confronted in his letters to the Churches. The Gnostics claimed that Jesus did not come in the flesh, but was only a spirit.

Gnosticism isn't merely an ancient heresy, but is very much alive and well today. In a Gnostic view, money is evil, sordid, filthy, etc. When people buy into this lie, "good" people seek to avoid money. Of course,

---

12   Doug Seebeck & Timothy Stoner, *My Business My Mission* (Grand Rapids, MI: Partners Worldwide, 2009), p. 89.

Gnosticism is dangerous for many other reasons, but to say that money is evil strips us of the possibility of using it for good.

Ironically, a result of Gnostic teaching argues that since only the spiritual world counts, it doesn't matter what we do in the material realm. As a result of this twisted thinking, Gnosticism often leads to licentious indulgence including all abuses imaginable.

Also, let's be clear that the phrase "Money is the root of evil" is not in the Bible. There's a verse very similar to that, but it has a *different* meaning. Paul explains in 1 Timothy 6:10, "For the *love* of money is a root of all kinds of evil, for which some have strayed from the faith in their greediness, and pierced themselves through with many sorrows." (My emphasis)

> *"The love of money as a possession—as distinguished from the love of money as a means to the enjoyments and realities of life—will be recognized for what it is, a somewhat disgusting morbidity, one of those semi-criminal, semi-pathological propensities which one hands over with a shudder to the specialists in mental disease."*
> **—John Maynard Keynes**

Money itself is good and useful to God and us. But a love for it turns it into something for which it was never intended. To *love* money is to pervert its good and proper purpose.

One of the most misunderstood incidents in the New Testament directly applies here. In Luke 18, we read about a wealthy young ruler who came to Jesus with a very important question, "Good Teacher, what shall I do to inherit eternal life?" But look at Jesus' response:

> *"Why do you call Me good? No one is good but One, that is, God. You know the commandments: 'Do not commit adultery,' 'Do not murder,' 'Do not steal,' 'Do not bear false witness,' 'Honor your*

father and your mother.'" And he said, "All these things I have kept
from my youth." So when Jesus heard these things, He said to him,
"You still lack one thing. Sell all that you have and distribute to
the poor, and you will have treasure in heaven; and come, follow
Me." But when he heard this, he became very sorrowful, for he
was very rich. And when Jesus saw that he became very sorrowful,
He said, "How hard it is for those who have riches to enter the
kingdom of God!"

—Luke 18:19-24

Many assume this incident is all about wealth and that if only this young man could've gotten rid of his wealth, he'd have been alright. But let's look more closely at what happened.

First, notice the way this young man approached Jesus and Jesus' response:

"Good Teacher, what shall I do to inherit eternal life?" So Jesus said
to him, "Why do you call Me good? No one is good but One, that
is, God."

Why do you suppose Jesus corrected the young man about calling Jesus good? Is Jesus denying that He is good? Absolutely not, because one of the conditions He gave this man to inherit eternal life was to follow Him. Instead, Jesus answered the rest of the young man's question by quoting five of the Ten Commandments. To which the young man replied, "All these things I have kept from my youth."

Part of this young man's problem was that he saw himself as "good" and Jesus subtly showed him otherwise. In fact, Jesus apparently left off the first four of the Ten Commandments deliberately. The ones He quoted all focus on how we treat other people. But the first four zero in on how we view and treat God.

Let's look at the first of the Ten Commandments. This young Jewish man would have known this commandment by heart. The fact that Jesus didn't recite it would've been blatantly clear. "I am the Lord your God, who brought you out of the land of Egypt, out of the house of bondage. You shall have no other gods before Me." (Exodus 20:2-3)

At this point, Jesus told this young man that he still lacked one thing. This was a test. If he passed the test, he would "inherit eternal life." Here was the test: "Sell all that you have and distribute to the poor, and you will have treasure in heaven; and come, follow Me."

In other words, the test was: "You must choose which you love more: Me or your riches!"

Jesus even promised him more than eternal life, but also "treasures in heaven." Jesus was offering this rich young man an upgrade. But sadly, the young man chose his riches over Jesus. This test revealed that wealth was his god. He was not keeping the first of Ten Commandments, the most basic of all. The thought of parting with his wealth to gain eternal fellowship with God was too much for him. He went away sad because Jesus showed him the truth of where his affections lay.

So, we see that this story is not primarily about money, but about our *affections*. That's why the Scriptures say that "The *love* of money is the root of all kinds of evil," and, "You cannot serve God and mammon." (Matthew 6:24)

Jesus went on to tell the young man, "How hard it is for those who have riches to enter the kingdom of God!" Why? Because they're inclined to put their trust in riches. It's easy for them to worship riches as their god. But ... this tendency is not merely common among the wealthy.

Paul told Timothy, "Those who *desire* to be rich fall into temptation and a snare, and into many foolish and harmful lusts which drown men in destruction and perdition. For the love of money is a root of all kinds of evil." (1 Timothy 6:9-10)

The dangers of *worshiping* money apply to anyone—wealthy, poor or anywhere in between. It's not money or wealth per se that gets us into trouble, but *love* for it, *trust* in it, and *worship* of it.

But it's also true that it's possible to steward wealth in a way that keeps money in its rightful place and honors God. In fact, we find such an example in the very next chapter in Luke's Gospel following the account of the rich young ruler.

In Luke 19, Jesus met a wealthy tax collector named Zacchaeus. Jesus went to his house for dinner and at some point during that meal, Zacchaeus was offered the same test that the rich young ruler had failed. But Zacchaeus passed the test with a commendation from Jesus. Here's what Zacchaeus said:

> *"Look, Lord, I give half of my goods to the poor; and if I have taken anything from anyone by false accusation, I restore fourfold." And Jesus said to him, "Today salvation has come to this house, because he also is a son of Abraham."*
> **—Luke 19:8-9**

What? Zacchaeus only gave *half* of his goods to the poor? You mean he got to keep the other half? Yes, and this underscores what we said earlier. It's never really about the money. It's about our *affections* and who or what we put our *trust* in. Zacchaeus chose to trust Jesus and follow Him.

Limiting Money Beliefs and the Liberating Truth About Each

Let's look at some common beliefs about money that may sound right, or contain a nugget of truth, but in fact are very *limiting* and untrue. We'll contrast each of those with a corresponding truth about money that is *liberating*.

Limiting Money Beliefs	Liberating Truths about Money
Money is the root of all evil.	Money is fundamentally good.
It takes money to make money.	Money is the reward for productive work.
Money doesn't grow on trees.	If you own an orchard it does. And the godly person is like a tree planted by streams of water, whatever they do prospers. (Psalm 1)
Money is dirty ("filthy rich").	God blesses us with wealth and possessions.
Poor is pure.	Purity only comes by walking with the King.
Wealthy people look down on poor people.	Pride and snobbery are not restricted to any social class.
Rich people don't get into heaven.	Rich people, like anyone else, must put their hope in God, not in riches.
Money isn't everything.	God gives us money to enjoy but not to worship.
The best things in life are free.	God richly gives us all things to enjoy. (1 Timothy 6:17)
"Normal" people resent rich people.	Resentment is not restricted to any social class.
You need a high level of education to make money.	Lack of education may sound like a good excuse, but it's no barrier to prosperity.
Money can't buy happiness.	We can be joyful and content regardless of our bank balance.
Money can't buy love.	Prosperity is often the product of love.

Money is a heavy burden.	Money weighs little for those accustomed to using it rightly. And it weighs little for those who recognize God as its rightful owner.
It takes hard work to make a lot of money.	Work enjoyed is not hard and yields prosperity.

Mindless Consumption: The Enemy of Productivity and Prosperity

Another way in which the war on prosperity hinders the mission of the church pertains to our understanding of prosperity itself.

For several decades, we Americans have been caught in a dangerous trap. We've come to equate *consumption* with *prosperity*. It's important to note that consumption, like money and business, is morally good and worthy: after all, if we don't consume, there is no one for the producers to sell to, and the whole system collapses. *Mindless* consumption is as different from *healthy* consumption as night from day. The two are diametrically opposed. Actually, *mindless* consumption hinders productivity and diminishes prosperity.

I define *mindless consumption* as the accumulation of consumer goods without careful thought, and with the primary intention of seeking the approval of other people. It is the pitiful attempt to feel important and worthy by measure of the opinions of the crowd. It is the abdication of one's own mind, in favor of the opinions of the mind of the mob.

Both philosophically and practically most of us view *consumption* and *prosperity* as synonymous. Or at the very least we see our consumption of goods and services as a visible indicator of our prosperity. This is mindless consumption. Consider the following examples.

In reality, median household incomes have been relatively flat for decades, in spite of the fact that there's been a sharp rise in dual income households. In other words, it now takes two of us in a household to bring home roughly the same amount of money.[13, 14]

Meanwhile, the average home size post WW2 in the U.S. was about 1100 sq. ft. In 1973 the average rose to 1525 sq. ft. and in 2015 the average U.S. home size jumped to 2687 sq. ft. During all those years, accounting for inflation, the average cost per square foot has remained constant at about $116. It's also interesting to note that the average size of a family has dropped considerably during that period as well.[15, 16]

My point is that we look at our nicer, larger, well-equipped homes and could easily conclude that we're better off than our parents or grandparents. But the truth is that we're just spending way more of our hard-earned paychecks on our homes than they did. This is not prosperity, but consumption and if anything, our high level of consumption has eaten away at our prosperity.

Robert Frank, economics professor at Cornell University, explains, "It is natural for people at all income levels to experience new desires in the presence of others who spend more than they do."[17] No doubt the media plays into the equation as well. As we see what the rich and famous are enjoying, we want it too. Consequently, we've found that we can "afford" those cruises, luxury cars, and expensive clothes by means of (and note their carefully chosen names): Discover Cards, MasterCards, and VISA.

---

13   FRED Economic Research, "Real Median Household Income in the United States," September 13, 2016, https://fred.stlouisfed.org/series/MEHOINUSA672N.

14   PEW Research Center, "The Rise in Dual Income Households," June 18, 2015, http://www.pewresearch.org/ft_dual-income-households-1960-2012-2/.

15   Mark J. Perry, "New US homes today are 1,000 square feet larger than in 1973 and living space per person has nearly doubled," June 5, 2016, http://www.aei.org/publication/new-us-homes-today-are-1000-square-feet-larger-than-in-1973-and-living-space-per-person-has-nearly-doubled/.

16   Robert H. Frank, *Luxury Fever: Why Money Fails to Satisfy in an Era of Excess* (New York, NY: The Free Press, 1999), p. 21.

17   Robert H. Frank, p. 10.

Our spending (consumption) has skyrocketed in contrast to our relatively flat incomes. What's the result?

- **Deep indebtedness.** Both as individuals and as a nation, we've become deeply in debt. We work for our creditors. Many live from paycheck to paycheck, barely able to make their minimum payments, a practice which almost guarantees a lifetime of debt.
- **Little savings.** As Americans, we save far less of our income than people in other affluent countries. As of first quarter 2017, our net savings as a percentage of gross national income was just 2.3 percent.[18] We'll say more about the relationship between saving and prosperity later.
- **Waning generosity.** According to an article in *Christianity Today*, American Evangelicals give a paltry 4 percent of their income.[19] Strapped with debt, we have little left over to give.
- **Less happiness.** Although there are sufficient studies to support the fact that having more stuff won't make us happier, no doubt we've all experienced this fact first-hand. Jesus said, "One's life does not consist in the abundance of the things he possesses." (Luke 12:15) And yet, we keep pursuing happiness by buying more stuff!

Reckless, unwise consumption erodes prosperity like nothing else.

Am I saying we should all live in shipping container "tiny houses," or live in voluntary poverty like the ancient Stoics, and never enjoy "the finer things"? By no means! But clearly many Americans have an unrealistically inflated idea of what they can afford. Buying things on

---

18 FRED Economic Research, "Net Savings as a Percentage of Gross National Income," May 26, 2017, https://fred.stlouisfed.org/series/W207RC1Q156SBEA.

19 Ruth Moon, "Are American Evangelicals Stingy?" *Christianity Today*, January 31, 2011,http://www.christianitytoday.com/ct/2011/february/areevangelicalsstingy.html.

credit cards with money we don't have, to impress people we don't really know (often our neighbors) or don't really like (sadly, this is often our own families), is not "healthy consumption." It is a recipe for financial disaster.

Now, I am not proposing there is anything wrong with having a nice car, house, wardrobe, etc.—if we can afford those things. If we want them because we appreciate and take pleasure in them (and not so that we can win the second-hand approval of other men's opinions), then go for it!

We desperately need to practice *intentional* and *wise* consumption. Such consumption requires building a certain level of wealth and financial health; requires paying for consumer goods outright and not with credit cards; and requires careful examination of our own motives.

In this chapter, we've seen that all these issues wage war against prosperity:

- The way we conduct business
- The outright interference of the devil
- Our misconceptions about money
- The war on the wealthy
- The Gnostic teaching that money is evil
- Our misplaced affections
- Our limiting money beliefs
- Confusing consumption with prosperity

We've also seen how this war against prosperity is hindering the mission of the church. Christ's mission was "to set the captives free. And this is the mission He gives anyone who says he or she wants to be His disciple and follow Him. 'Become like me,' I believe He is saying, 'set the captives free, and if it will require you to break the power of pervasive cultural, spiritual, demonic strongholds, then by all means do that as well.'"[20]

Let me be clear: lifting people out of poverty is not the crux of the gospel message. Jesus Christ came to save us from our sins, reconcile us with the Father, and wrest control of the earth from the "principalities and powers."[21] He came to initiate a revolution. That revolutionary life begins here and now on earth. His resurrection power is effective to break the bonds of poverty as well as any other social ill. If we cannot work toward that and demonstrate it in Christ's name, then our mission (the church's mission) is hindered.

---

20 Doug Seebeck, p. 73.
21 N.T. Wright, *The Day the Revolution Began*

Chapter 5

The Perils of Prosperity

•••••••●••••••••

The distortions of something good must not cause us to think that the thing itself is evil. Money is good in itself, and provides us many opportunities for glorifying God.

—Wayne Grudem

S o far, we've argued that business and its natural by-products: productivity and prosperity, are all essentially good and gifts from God. We've seen plenty of examples in which God has blessed people with prosperity.

At the same time, prosperity brings peril in the same way accepting any great responsibility does. In this chapter, we want to turn our attention to the dangers and pitfalls of prosperity and how to avoid them. We'll look at the risks and rewards of building wealth—why God wants you to prosper—but only when you are "safe for success."

10 Wealth Warnings

Money is fundamentally good, but like all other good things God has given us, it's possible to pervert and abuse money. The Scriptures offer numerous warnings about such abuse and perversion. Here are just a few:

1. **Money Is God's Number One Rival for Our Affections.** "No one can serve two masters; for either he will hate the one and love the other, or else he will be loyal to the one and despise the other. You cannot serve God and mammon." (Matthew 6:24).

   Idolatry was Israel's downfall. John urged his readers to keep themselves from idols (1 John 5:21). For most of us, idolatry seems like something from ancient times or that only occurs in "pagan" lands, so idolatry isn't even on our radar. But Jesus identified money as the chief competitor for our affections and worship of God. The idol of money is as real and relevant today as ever and brings with it significant danger (1 Timothy 6:9).

   One of the writers of the Proverbs was so concerned about the dangers of wealth that he earnestly prayed this prayer:

   Give me neither poverty nor riches—Feed me with the food allotted to me; Lest I be full and deny You, and say, "Who is the Lord?" Or lest I be poor and steal, and profane the name of my God. –Proverbs 30:7-9

   This isn't a prescription for each of us to be neither poor nor rich, by the way. It does highlight the importance of knowing how susceptible we are to the allure of wealth as an idol, and to avoid being in situations that tempt us beyond our endurance. In other words, if you're an alcoholic, a bar is the wrong place to go for a hamburger.

2. **Wealth Gained by Dishonest Means Leads to Poverty.**
"Wealth gained by dishonesty will be diminished, but he who gathers by labor will increase." (Proverbs 13:11) Riches obtained in this manner damage both the recipient and others. Also, we must not assume that this is a rare or infrequent problem. James warned his wealthy readers:

> *Come now, you rich, weep and howl for your miseries that are coming upon you! Your riches are corrupted, and your garments are moth-eaten. Your gold and silver are corroded, and their corrosion will be a witness against you and will eat your flesh like fire. You have heaped up treasure in the last days. Indeed the wages of the laborers who mowed your fields, which you kept back by fraud, cry out; and the cries of the reapers have reached the ears of the Lord of Sabbath. You have lived on the earth in pleasure and luxury; you have fattened your hearts as in a day of slaughter. You have condemned, you have murdered the just; he does not resist you.*
>
> **—James 5:1-6**

Who is James talking to here? Only the ultra-wealthy perhaps? Is he only addressing the top 1% of people in the world? Well here's the shocking truth: that includes almost every one of us in the developed world, and certainly almost everyone in the United States of America!

In fact the median family income in the USA is $55,575.[22] According to the Global Rich List, a website that calculates how "rich" you are based on your income (as compared to the rest of the world), an income of $55,575 puts you in the top 0.23% richest people in the world by income.

---

22 https://en.wikipedia.org/wiki/Household_income_in_the_United_States.

We're so rich, we're not in the top 1%—we're in the top .23%! That makes the passage from James feel a bit more personal, doesn't it?

How can we honor God by maintaining a good reputation in the world if we engage in shady business practices? In our work, it's not just our reputation or our company's reputation at stake, but God's.

3. **There Is No Security in Wealth.** King David, a man who rose from being a shepherd boy to becoming Israel's greatest king, wrote, "If riches increase, do not set your heart on them." (Psalm 62:10) And his son, Solomon, perhaps one of the wealthiest men that ever lived, warned, "He who trusts in his riches will fall." (Proverbs 11:28)

No matter how much or little money we have, our hope and trust must be in the Lord, not in our bank account. Paul instructed Timothy, "Command those who are rich in this present age not to be haughty, nor to trust in uncertain riches but in the living God, who gives us richly all things to enjoy. Let them do good, that they be rich in good works, ready to give, willing to share." (1 Timothy 6:17–18)

One of the ways I've noticed that this temptation creeps up on us looks something like this. Whether due to our spending habits or unforeseen expenses, we run out of money before the end of the month. So what do we do? All too often, instead of either going without or trusting God for our needs, we simply pull out the credit card. Unwittingly, we look to our credit card to meet our needs instead of God.

Of course, there's a double-whammy when we do that! Not only have we failed to trust God for our needs, but we've put ourselves in a worse situation by increasing our debt. If there's no security in wealth, then we certainly don't find it in unwise borrowing!

> *The rich rules over the poor, and the borrower is the slave of the lender.*
> **—Proverbs 22:7 (ESV)**

4. **Equal Distribution of Wealth Helps No One.** We've already seen how the master in Jesus' parable of the talents distributed funds to each servant "according to his ability." (Matthew 25:14–30) Even when speaking of grace, God says He gives different gifts and varying degrees of grace to each person (Romans 12:6).

   The theory that a society can distribute wealth equally among its members has been attempted in various forms of Communism in many different countries, at various times and in a variety of ways. It has never worked under any circumstances. Equal distribution of wealth diminishes wealth and prosperity among all and creates an even greater rift between the very wealthy and the have-nots.

   No matter which side of wealth you find yourself on, don't make the mistake of thinking that equally distributing wealth is the answer.

5. **Feigned Prosperity.** Have you ever driven through a poorer part of town and wondered how these people can afford to be driving nice, new cars? But wait, we don't have to go to the poorer parts of town to observe this. It's on display all around us.

   Robert Frank explains, "When people at the top spend more, others just below them will inevitably spend more also, and so on all the way down the economic ladder."[23] We want

---

23 Robert H. Frank, p. 11.

to look successful. We want to appear prosperous, so we buy things we can't afford to impress people we don't even know.

What are we trying to prove when we fake a level of prosperity that isn't ours? If anything, we alienate others, and place undue stress on our budget.

6. **It's Okay to Own Things, But Not Okay to Be Owned by Things.** Jesus warned, "One's life does not consist in the abundance of the things he possesses." (Luke 12:15) More and better stuff will not make us happier. And the desire for more can easily distract us and lead us astray.

First we become a slave to our desires. Then, we become a slave to our indebtedness. We hear the alluring voice of our culture that calls out, "Come on, splurge! You owe it to yourself. You've earned this." The problem is, we haven't *earned* it, but will be paying for it for many years to come.

7. **Envy, Jealousy, and Covetousness Eat Away at Us Like Cancer.** The Tenth Commandment instructs us not to covet anyone else's possessions. Envy, jealousy and covetousness are emotional responses that not only hurt others but consume us. These evil responses breed even more insidious sins. Envy and jealousy drove Cain to kill his brother Abel.

Today, we've euphemized covetousness by calling it "keeping up with the Jones'." Desire for more—especially when it belongs to someone else—is a deadly trap to avoid at all costs. Instead, rejoice with others over their blessings and learn contentment.

Once again, James tackles this topic head-on:

Where do wars and fights come from among you? Do they not come from your desires for pleasure that war in your members? You lust and do not have. You murder and covet and cannot obtain. You fight and war. Yet you do not have because you do not ask. You ask and do not receive, because you ask amiss, that you may spend it on your pleasures.

—James 4:1-3

8. **"Get Rich Quick" Schemes that Promise Wealth Are a Curse.** "A faithful man will abound with blessings, but he who hastens to be rich will not go unpunished." (Proverbs 28:20)

A Time Magazine article published in 2016 follows the experiences of lottery winners.[24] The article explains that most lottery winners end up *broke* and *miserable* within a few years of receiving their windfall.

Don McNay, a financial consultant to lottery winners and the author of *Life Lessons from the Lottery,* refers to winning the lottery as a "curse that makes people's lives worse," not better.[25] I believe that most lottery winners, or those who come into large sums of money which they did not produce, have never learned how to properly handle such funds. As a result, it would be like a 12-year-old child taking the reins as CEO of a large corporation. It's a recipe for disaster!

It may be human nature to always seek the easy way out, but the problem is that path doesn't build character. The writer of Hebrews spoke to this issue when he wrote, "All discipline for the moment seems not to be joyful, but sorrowful; yet to those who have been trained by it, afterwards it yields the peaceful fruit of righteousness." (Hebrews 12:11 NASB)

9. **Wealth Can Lead to Pride and Ingratitude.** As the Children of Israel stood on the border of Canaan, ready to be ushered in by Joshua, God gave them a very strong warning:

---

24 Melissa Chan, "Here's How Winning the Lottery Makes You Miserable," Time, January 12, 2016, http://time.com/4176128/powerball-jackpot-lottery-winners/.
25 Melissa Chan.

When you have eaten and are full, then you shall bless the Lord your God for the good land which He has given you. Beware that you do not forget the Lord your God by not keeping His commandments, His judgments, and His statutes which I command you today, lest—when you have eaten and are full, and have built beautiful houses and dwell in them; and when your herds and your flocks multiply, and your silver and your gold are multiplied, and all that you have is multiplied; when your heart is lifted up, and you forget the Lord your God who brought you out of the land of Egypt, from the house of bondage... then you say in your heart, "My power and the might of my hand have gained me this wealth."

Remember the Lord your God, for it is He who gives you power to get wealth, that He may establish His covenant which He swore to your fathers, as it is this day.

—Deuteronomy 8:10-14, 17

Prosperity and wealth can make us feel important, proud, and self-sufficient. It becomes easy to take credit for all we have and enjoy, forgetting that it is God who has graciously blessed with all things. Unfortunately, Israel did not heed God's warning. Will we?

10. **Wealth and Prosperity Can Make Us Complacent.** Jesus told a very sobering parable in Luke 12:16-21 that addresses this temptation:

Then He spoke a parable to them, saying: "The ground of a certain rich man yielded plentifully. And he thought within himself, saying, 'What shall I do, since I have no room to store my crops?' So he said, 'I will do this: I will pull down my barns and build greater, and there I will store all my crops and my goods. And I will say to my soul, "Soul, you have many goods laid up for many years; take your ease; eat, drink, and be merry.'" But God said to him, 'Fool! This night your soul will be required of you; then whose will those things be which you have provided?'

"So is he who lays up treasure for himself, and is not rich toward God."

What's so sobering about this parable is how accurately it describes the "American dream" of retirement! Notice that Jesus' indictment on this rich man is not because of his wealth, but his preoccupation with it. His financial picture had no room for God or anyone else. He merely saw his wealth as a means for taking his ease and indulging himself with pleasures—he saw it as his ultimate and only source of fulfillment. He had eliminated from his life the joy of productivity and work well-done, and He had forgotten God, who gave him the power to create the wealth to begin with.

We also see from this parable that it's quite possible to experience the blessing and prosperity of God, but then to manage it in a way that neither honors God nor oneself.

With all the potential dangers surrounding money, wealth and prosperity, we might wonder whether it's even possible to experience wealth and come away unscathed! But as Wayne Grudem points out, "The distortions of something good must not cause us to think that the thing itself is evil. Money is good in itself, and provides us many opportunities for *glorifying* God."[26] [Emphasis mine.]

In the chapters that follow, we'll look more closely at some of these opportunities with which we can glorify God with money.

---

26 Wayne Grudem, p. 50.

Chapter 6

What Is Prosperity?

•••••••••●•••••••••

And Jabez called on the God of Israel saying, "Oh, that You would bless me indeed, and enlarge my territory, that Your hand would be with me, and that You would keep me from evil, that I may not cause pain!" So God granted him what he requested.
—1 Chronicles 4:10

Prosperity Is a Mindset

You may wonder why I've waited until now to define *prosperity*. But my intent was to lead you to this conclusion little by little rather than simply hit you over the head with it from the beginning.

The dictionary defines *prosperity* as, "a successful, flourishing, or thriving condition, especially in financial respects."[27] Granted, we typically think of prosperity in financial terms. But both the Bible and

---

27   Dictionary.com, "prosperity."

our own experience show that prosperity is dependent on a whole lot more than money.

Consider Proverbs 15:16 for instance, "Better is a little with the fear of the Lord, than great treasure with trouble." We could paraphrase that verse like this: "Our prosperity has far more to do with our relationship with God than great treasures." As I write that, I'm reminded of what Jesus said, "For what profit is it to a man if he gains the whole world, and loses his own soul? Or what will a man give in exchange for his soul?" (Matthew 16:26)

I'm not saying that prosperity has nothing to do with money or finances, but there are matters in addition to wealth that determine full, abundant prosperity.

King Solomon describes another one of those matters in Proverbs 16:8, "Better is a little with righteousness, than vast revenues without justice." In other words, someone may have vast revenues, but if they can't experience justice, they'd be better off (i.e., more prosperous) with righteousness and only meager funds.

The Link Between Contentment and Prosperity

Prosperity truly is a mindset, an attitude of the heart, a sense of well-being. Let me demonstrate this in another way. In Philippians, Paul shared with that church, "I have learned in whatever state I am, to be content: I know how to be abased, and I know how to abound. Everywhere and in all things I have learned both to be full and to be hungry, both to abound and to suffer need." (Philippians 4:11-12)

There's a strong link between contentment and prosperity. One might even say that we cannot experience prosperity apart from contentment. I think that's basically what Paul is saying here. For in Christ's strength (Philippians 4:13) he has learned how to be content both when he had more than he needed and when he was in great need.

Contentment is a state of satisfaction. When we are content, we are at peace—without anxiety or stress. When we are content, we feel prosperous regardless of the state of our finances. And by the way, it's good to remind ourselves here that prosperity is relative. There is no set dollar amount that establishes the prosperity threshold, "You have now reached prosperity."

From this perspective, imagine two people. They both make the same amount of money. Their basic expenses for living are the same. They don't make enough to buy things they would like to have. Instead, they barely get by each month. One of these individuals is content in their financial situation, the other is miserable. Which one is prospering? Is either of them prospering? Chances are, the one who is content would express with gratitude that they have all they need. They feel prosperous. Certainly the other one does not.

Or, consider two other individuals. These individuals both make high, seven-figure incomes. They both live in very nice homes in the best part of town. They drive new cars for which they paid cash. One of them is content, the other is miserable because he only sees that some others have more than he, and he will not be content until his wealth outstrips those people as well. I contend that while they're both prosperous, the one who is malcontent doesn't *feel* prosperous and cannot enjoy his prosperity in his discontented frame of mind.

King Solomon maintained this line of thinking when he wrote, "He who loves silver will not be satisfied with silver; nor he who loves abundance, with increase." (Ecclesiastes 5:10) What good is prosperity if one can't enjoy it? In fact, if one is discontented, chances are they won't consider themselves prosperous. They certainly aren't experiencing "a successful, flourishing, or thriving condition."

King Solomon speaks of this again, "As for every man to whom God has given riches and wealth, and given him power to eat of it, to receive his heritage and rejoice in his labor—this is the gift of God." (Ecclesiastes 5:19) We see once again from this passage that prosperity consists of far more than wealth. In the mind of its owner, prosperity doesn't exist unless they can enjoy it. And even the ability to enjoy one's prosperity is a gift of God.

Coming to Grips with Our Prosperity

As we've already seen, in Christ and as children of Abraham we are heirs of the world. In this life, we are like children of a very wealthy father. We have not yet come of age to receive our inheritance, but it is there just waiting for us. It is real, and it is certain. So from our current "spiritual" situation in Christ, we are wealthy beyond comprehension.

In Paul's letter to the church in Ephesus he told them that he prayed for them non-stop:

> *That the God of our Lord Jesus Christ, the Father of glory, may give to you the spirit of wisdom and revelation in the knowledge of Him, the eyes of your understanding being enlightened; that you may know what is the hope of His calling, what are the riches of the glory of His inheritance in the saints, and what is the exceeding greatness of His power toward us who believe, according to the working of His mighty power.*
> **—Ephesians 1:18-19**

This is vital! Paul was praying for them incessantly that the Lord would give them "the spirit of wisdom and revelation in the knowledge of Him." Why? Among other things, so they could see "what are the riches of the glory of His inheritance in the saints."

Why was it so important to Paul that his readers grasp the magnitude of their inheritance? Because an understanding of our prosperous stance in the Lord radically impacts the way we live today. Truly grasping the reality of our inheritance in Christ impacts our relationship with God, with people, with His church, with our work, with our finances, and virtually every other area of our lives.

"Eye has not seen, nor ear heard, nor have entered into the heart of man the things which God has prepared for those who love Him." (1 Corinthians 2:9) Try to imagine all that God has prepared for you in your inheritance with Christ for all eternity. Try real hard! You can't do it! We cannot fully grasp or even imagine all that God has prepared for us! Wow! Amazing!

Yet, in the very next verse he writes, "But God has revealed them to us through His Spirit." What we don't have the human potential to begin to grasp cognitively, the Holy Spirit is revealing to us. He's giving us a peek into the future of the magnitude and extent of our prosperity in Christ.

Don't be fooled into thinking it's only about gold, silver and jewels. Full prosperity comes in the context of the loving relationship we enjoy with our infinite Father. He alone gives us our capacity for contentment, joy, and peace. We are utterly satisfied in His presence—not because of what He *gives* us, but because we're *with* Him—for all eternity. And eternity starts right now. Not in some distant future. Not in some ethereal "other world." Right here. Right now.

In the words of that great Christian philosopher, Francis Schaeffer, "How shall we then live?" Given what the Holy Spirit has revealed to us about our inheritance in Christ, how shall we live? How does this truth impact us? What difference does our inheritance in Christ make in our lives right now?

First and foremost, we want to live in a manner worthy of our calling as His children. We should desire to please Him in all things, not in order to *obtain* our inheritance, but because He has *already* freely *given* it.

As dearly loved children, we want to serve Him. We want to express our enjoyment of Him. For "God is most glorified in us, when we are most satisfied in Him,"[28] writes John Piper. He refers to this as "Christian hedonism." It's what the church fathers described as the "chief end of man:" that is "To glorify God and enjoy Him forever."[29]

"The only way to glorify the all-sufficiency of God is to come to Him because in His presence is fullness of joy and at His right hand are pleasures for evermore (Psalm 16:11)."[30]

In view of our inheritance, our response to God is simply to enjoy His presence. We bask in His great love, mercy, goodness, and faithfulness. We truly enjoy our prosperity in Him. Our chief joy is in the Giver not His gifts.

This does not mean there is no joy in His gifts! Think how insulting it would be if, when handed a gift that cost the Giver his very life, you threw it on the ground and pronounced it worthless—or worse, called it "evil" and "filthy."

You see, there is a very real, here-and-now prosperity that we can experience as well. And I believe that our grasp of our eternal inheritance plays a huge role in how we deal with prosperity in the here and now.

Two Traps

"Money isn't everything, as long as you have enough."
—Malcolm Forbes

I see two traps that await those who wish to follow Jesus and who experience the kind of "success" that He offers.

Those traps are the twin perils of *poverty* and *greed*.

---

28   John Piper, *The Dangerous Duty of Delight* (Sisters, OR: Multnomah Publishers, Inc., 2001), p. 20.
29   The Westminster Catechism.
30   John Piper, p. 38.

Right now, these two mindsets hold the world in their power—especially so in the realm of business and online marketing; they are the source of the economic woes we see all around us today.

The poverty mindset is a product of *fear*. This is the kind of fear that tells you there will never be enough. This fear threatens that in order for me to win, someone else has to lose; and that disaster is always around the corner. That doesn't sound like a very pleasant way to live, now does it?

The poverty mindset will keep you broke, in debt, and fearful for the rest of your life if you don't denounce it.

The other enemy of true prosperity is the greed mindset. This is the mindset of second-hand identity, of deriving one's value by the standards of others, and of making oneself feel better by putting others down. This is the mindset that leads people to collect as many boats, cars, gigantic houses, and material possessions *as a way of proving their own value as a person.* This mindset is also motivated by fear: *the fear of not being valued by others.*

These two mindsets, greed and poverty lead to the actual sins of "you rich," which are contained in that passage from James. Was the actual sin of those rich people simply being rich, or something else? Read the passage again, with some phrases emphasized for clarity:

> You have heaped up treasure in the last days. Indeed **the wages of the laborers who mowed your fields, which you kept back by fraud,** cry out; and the cries of the reapers have reached the ears of the Lord of Sabbath. You have lived on the earth in pleasure and luxury; you have fattened your hearts as in a day of slaughter. **You have condemned, you have murdered the just.**

Is the picture becoming a bit clearer?

The Apostle Paul clarifies the matter even further. Writing to his protégé, Timothy, he tells the younger pastor how to instruct the rich among his congregation:

> *Command those who are rich in this present age **not to be haughty, nor to trust in uncertain riches but in the living God,** who gives us richly all things to enjoy. **Let them do good, that they be rich in good works, ready to give, willing to share,** storing up for themselves a good foundation for the time to come, that they may lay hold on eternal life.*
> —1 Timothy 6:17-19

Notice **he does not command them to stop being rich**. He commands:

- "Not to be haughty"
- "Nor to trust in uncertain riches but in the living God"
- "Let them do good"
- "Be ready to give"
- "Be willing to share"

It's Okay to Be Rich—But First Seek God's Kingdom

Paul is not shaming or guilting people for being rich. Instead, he seems to be instructing us (because most of us reading this *are* among the richest people in the world) about how to live if we are rich.

A proper relationship with our wealth cannot be determined by the size of our house or the kind of cars we drive. Merely having nice possessions is not an indicator of the condition of someone's soul.

But neither is having very few possessions a measure of spiritual health. Just because someone does not experience financial abundance in one moment in time does not mean that they are a slave to poverty.

Likewise, being focused on material possessions for the wrong reasons can lead to pride, and tempt one to become greedy.

My point is simply this: the external circumstances are never a reliable indicator of the condition of a person's heart.

But from the standpoint of guarding yourself against great unhappiness, I caution you to avoid both of these deadly mindsets. Stay far away from the poverty mindset, and have faith that even when you are temporarily in lack, there will always be enough. There is always more of everything you need available to you, because your heavenly Father will provide.

Likewise, you should strenuously avoid falling in love with material possessions acquired for the sake of stoking your pride. Piling up "stuff" to prove your own value to others is a quick road to misery. What others think of you is no concern of yours.

· · · · · · · · ● · · · · · · · · ·

What others think of you is no concern of yours.

· · · · · · · · ● · · · · · · · · ·

When you can navigate successfully and stay out of these two mindsets—when you are slave to neither greed nor poverty—you experience what God wants for you with all His heart. You experience full prosperity.

The Apostle Paul said that he had learned the secret to being content whether he had much (which he sometimes did) or whether he had nothing (a condition he also experienced frequently). What was his secret? The same secret I've been talking to you about all along: he said, "I can do all things through Christ who strengthens me."

Be Safe for Success

As an entrepreneur, the primary aim of being in business is to create revenue. How do we do that? We offer a product or service to the market that solves a problem or serves a need. And we do so in such a way that our company makes a profit. This is common sense.

Where Christian entrepreneurs sometimes get lost is forgetting that the primary aim of their life is not to simply pile up as much money as possible. Your purpose is not to be a participant in a cosmic contest to see who can get the biggest stack of gold. No, the primary aim of the Christian entrepreneur's life is to glorify God (which means "to show His goodness"). And one of the ways God has called and gifted you to glorify Him is through entrepreneurship. For those who are truly called to the entrepreneurial life, this means seeking to run a successful (prosperous) business.

In order to fulfill God's purpose for our life as entrepreneurs and small business owners, it is necessary that we have a proper relationship between our heart and money. God clearly says in His Word that we cannot serve both God and money. What is not so obvious to many people is we can serve God *with our money,* and that doing so represents a proper heart-relationship toward money. In this way, we become "safe for success."

We must function "safe for success"—not giving in to greed and pride. We must succeed in a way that honors Jesus. It means not making money our idol. God is not against us having money, but He is against money having us.

Let's take a closer look at the passage I alluded to above. In Matthew 6:24, Jesus said:

No one can serve two masters; for either he will hate the one and love the other, or else he will be loyal to the one and despise the other. You cannot serve God and mammon.

"*No one* can serve *two* masters." The language Jesus used here was no doubt very deliberate. He is casting our relationship as one of a slave with a master. A slave only belongs to one master. Either we're in bondage to God or we're in bondage to money. Either we work to serve God as our master, or we work to serve money. It's one or the other… period!

In spite of the clarity of Jesus' words, we are tempted to think something like, "Okay, I'll serve God *primarily* and only direct a small portion of my efforts in serving money." No. You can't do it. You can't serve two masters. It's not a matter of priority, balance, or some other such nonsense. It's a matter of singular focus, affection and devotion.

••••••••••●••••••••••

Choosing to serve God rather than money is not a matter of priority, it's a matter of loyalty.

••••••••••●••••••••••

In fact, using the slave/master metaphor from God's perspective is a matter of ownership. We belong to Him. Will we faithfully serve Him, or rebel to serve another master?

If we choose to serve money even a little, we become enslaved to it and oust God as the Master in our life. And by the way, God is a gracious, loving, benevolent Master. Money, on the other hand, which was never designed to fill the role of a master, is harsh, cruel and demanding. If you've ever tried serving money, you know what I mean.

With God as your Master and money as tool, or a trust that you steward, you will keep money moving, you will pay fair wages, you will make square business deals, and you will enrich the lives of your employees, your customers, your vendors and the world at large. That is truly a formula for prosperity.

- Put your trust in God, not riches.
- Pursue God, not wealth.
- Expect productive work to produce prosperity.
- Be a good steward and generous with all that God entrusts to you.
- Learn contentment whether you have much or little.
- Contentment does not mean you have no goals or ambitions. Contentment is healthy; complacency is death.

Part II

LOVING PEOPLE: THE PURPOSE OF PROSPERITY

Many of us have been taught something like this: "It's okay for you to make a lot of money, as long as you give it all away to charity, or even better, to the church."

In this section of the book, I'd like to discuss with you God's purpose behind prosperity.

Business, commerce, and yes, even capitalism, were all God's idea first. Doing business and building wealth are, in and of themselves, inherently good, moral, and spiritual practices.

Business improves our lives, provides jobs and opportunities, and creates new stores of wealth that flow through the economy. All of these represent God-glorifying ways of loving people.

> *"A powerful cultural lie needs to be exposed and renounced: that it is God's will for the poor to be poor. But the rich are also being held hostage by beliefs that are equally false and just as oppressive: 'When I sell my business, I am going to go into ministry,' or, 'My job is to make as much money as I can in order to fund good ministries.' These comments are based on the lie that business people cannot engage in significant work for the Kingdom through business."*
> **—Doug Seebeck**

Chapter 7

Money Itself Has No Value[31]

● ● ● ● ● ● ● ● ● ● ● ● ● ● ● ● ●

"Small things are small things, but faithfulness with a small thing is a big thing."
—**Hudson Taylor**, 19th Century Missionary to China

Money is a good servant, a dangerous master.
—**Francis Bacon**

B elieve it or not, the way we view money determines how we can love people by means of it.

Most people think money is finite. Meaning there is a limited amount of wealth in the world. This gives rise to the idea that for some to be rich others must be poor. Basically, if a few people own 90% of the pie, then everyone else must live off the crumbs, which doesn't seem fair at all.

---

31 Sean Edwards is my son, and is gifted communicator in his own realm (politics and government). Sean agreed to contribute this chapter at my request. He does a beautiful job of clarifying the true nature of money. You will find more of Sean's work at his website, SeanEdwards.com. –Ray Edwards

And they are right. That wouldn't be fair!

Fortunately, though, this isn't how things work.

This understanding of money is fundamentally flawed. And it keeps people poor (rather than helping them).

What most people don't realize is that money itself has no value. It isn't real. I will prove it to you.

And once we realize that money doesn't have any real value, we can end world poverty.

Money Represents Our Labor

Despite what many believe, money is nothing more than an advanced barter system. In a barter system, we trade our services with each other in a way that helps all parties. If I'm a farmer and I need wool for clothing, then I will trade my apples with a shepherd for wool. I need wool, and the shepherd needs food. Everyone is happy.

But this system gets unwieldy very quickly. If I need wool, but the shepherd doesn't need apples, then I must go find someone who makes what he needs—and who wants apples. So, I trade with them, and then come back to the shepherd to trade for wool. Obviously, this system becomes very complex and we'd all spend all our time trying to find those who want what we've got to offer.

Fortunately, humans are geniuses and we figured out a better way: If everyone trades their products or services in for one item that everyone else values, then we can all trade with each other much easier. For instance, if everyone values gold, I can trade my apples for gold, which I can then use to trade with anyone for anything—even if they don't need apples.

This "trade medium" streamlines how we interact with each other. In a nutshell, money is that trade medium and represents our labor so that we can trade our products and services for anything with anyone.

The important point is this: Dollars, gold coins, and Euros do not have value in and of themselves. They only have value because we, as a society, have agreed that they can represent our labor. We've assigned value to money, that's the only reason it has value.

Money's Value Is Subjective

Even though we have agreed that money can represent our labor, its purchasing power (what money can buy) is not set in stone. Purchasing power fluctuates based on how we value things. In this sense, money's value is entirely subjective.

When we shop, we are constantly deciding if something is worth the price. We are asking, "Is this product worth the labor I expended for the money?"

We face this choice all the time. And it is why we buy different things at different prices. It is why markets fluctuate. It is why gas prices go up and down. It is why new cars are more expensive than old cars.

The takeaway is this: The value of money only exists in our heads. It only has value because I have decided that my money is worth the product or service I am purchasing. And the person from whom I am buying has decided that the amount of money I give them is worth the cost of creating their product or service. We have decided it is a fair trade. Our agreement is the only reason money has value.

Money Is Imaginary

This leads to a startling conclusion: Money exists because we've assigned worth or value to it. Money in and of itself has no intrinsic value.

If you don't believe me, consider a culture in which shells or beads are the monetary currency. Now try buying something at Sears or Kohl's with beads or shells. I think you get my point!

Even though the number of dollars in the world may be real and finite at any given point in time, the value we assign to those dollars is completely arbitrary. It changes all the time.

So, the wealth those dollars represent fluctuates and changes based on what we do or create.

Real wealth rests in our creative labor.

We add wealth to the world by building someone a house. We add wealth to the world by teaching children mathematics. We add wealth to the world by creating a faster computer that makes life easier.

We build wealth by creating. We generate wealth by making something of greater value from something of lesser value. We produce wealth by taking an idea and making it a reality. This is real wealth.

Money is not real wealth, because as we've seen it doesn't have intrinsic value. It only *represents* what we have created. And as soon as we decide that it can no longer represent our labor, it will be worthless.

> *For what profit is it to a man if he gains the whole world, and loses his own soul? Or what will a man give in exchange for his soul?*
> **—Matthew 16:26**

Wealth Is Limitless

This means that wealth is unlimited. Wealth is only limited by our ability to create. Meaning, if people decide not to create (i.e., work), then wealth is capped. But there is no physical or real limit on wealth.

Money does not limit our wealth. We limit wealth by how we think about money.

Our Policies Keep People Poor

Returning to our pie analogy, most of our laws are based on a zero-sum paradigm. Welfare programs, minimum wage laws, and many of other assistance programs are based on this idea.

We are saying that the rich (businesses, corporations, and the wealthy) need to give up some of the pie so that the rest of us have more to live on. It isn't fair that they have 90% of the pie when the rest of us are just trying to get by.

This whole paradigm is blind to the fact that money doesn't possess real (or actual, or intrinsic) value—and that wealth is unlimited! It is flawed and is hamstringing our country!

When we enact policies based on this zero-sum framework, we are not creating wealth. We are taking it from some and giving it to others. In fact, we are penalizing those who are wealthy for being wealthy! (This is the thinking behind the ideology of the redistribution of wealth.)

Putting aside the immorality of legalized theft, this *keeps people poor.*

This does not create more wealth. It just moves it around. And it inhibits wealth creation by reducing the capital creators who must create more wealth. As we've seen in our society, it also stifles any creativity that the have-nots could exercise to create wealth. Why should they work when they can make a better living by staying on Welfare?

In the short term, Welfare may seem like a good idea. And it may even temporarily address some very real social ills. But in the long run, it hurts everyone by inhibiting wealth creation.

If we let wealth creators make more wealth, they will generate more jobs and everyone will prosper. This is what has launched the massive explosion in prosperity in the last 200 years.

What Do We Do Now?

Welfare programs are built on the zero-sum fallacy. And when a house is built on a faulty foundation, you can't fix it. You must tear it down and rebuild it with a stronger foundation.

The sad part of this is that we are perpetuating the very thing we are trying to get rid of: poverty.

These policies are not increasing prosperity in the world. They are inhibiting it. The only way we can get rid of poverty is to create more wealth (and to teach the poor to do so as well). That is it. As Wayne Grudem rightly asserts, *"The only long-term solution to world poverty is business."*[32]

This is the only path to true prosperity for everyone on the planet. And this is good news!

It means that everyone can be prosperous. This is not a zero-sum game! No one has to be poor.

But to see that happen, we must realize one thing: , Money has no intrinsic value.

I'll leave you with these questions:

1. How many of your thoughts on money are based on the "zero-sum fallacy"? Are those thoughts helping or hindering you?

2. How can you create wealth in your personal life? Is it through a job where you get paid to help a business generate wealth? Or can you "create something out of nothing" and generate your own wealth?

3. What are three things that you can do to start generating more wealth in the next 30 days?

---

32 Wayne Grudem, p. 80.

Chapter 8

Money Won't Make You Rich, and Poverty Won't Make You Righteous

• • • • • • • • ● • • • • • • •

Stewardship is not really so much about what you give but what you allow yourself to keep.

—Milt Kuyers

Money is never the issue. Neither are possessions. Having much or having little makes no difference. It's the position of your heart as it relates to money. As we've already seen, true prosperity is a mindset. And discovering your true treasure is the key to prosperity.

When Jesus told the rich young ruler to sell all he had and give to the poor, in return He promised him: eternal life, treasure in heaven, and fellowship with Jesus (God). Unfortunately, this man was blind to what the Lord was saying to him. He couldn't see past his *stuff.* He could've had an upgrade in so many respects.

C.S. Lewis spoke to this issue in his book *The Weight of Glory:*

We are half-hearted creatures, fooling about with drink and sex and ambition when infinite joy is offered us, like an ignorant child who wants to go on making mud pies in a slum because he cannot imagine what is meant by the offer of a holiday at the sea. We are far too easily pleased.[33]

Commenting on the above passage, John Piper writes, "The problem with human beings is that we are far too easily pleased. We don't seek pleasure with nearly the resolve and passion that we should. And so we settle for mud pies of appetite instead of infinite delight."[34]

What Piper and Lewis are talking about is the infinite joy and pleasure available to us in God. King David understood this secret to true prosperity. Consider his words in Psalm 37:4, "Delight yourself also in the Lord, and He shall give you the desires of your heart." What does this mean? How do we "delight ourselves in the Lord"?

With the *childish* mentality of making mud pies in a slum, we might read that verse as a "blank-check" invitation to indulge in all our worldly wants and desires. That if we delight ourselves in the Lord (whatever that means), then He'll give us *anything* we want.

Consider this: Jesus plainly told His disciples that whatever they asked in His name would be granted to them.[35] Yet shortly after telling them they would receive anything they asked for in His name, he flatly denied a direct request! Here's what happened: a Samaritan village rejected Jesus, so James and John wanted to annihilate them:

And when His disciples James and John saw this, they said, "Lord, do You want us to command fire to come down from heaven and consume them, just as Elijah did?"

---

33 C. S. Lewis, *The Weight of Glory and Other Addresses* (Grand Rapids, MI: Eerdmans, 1965), pp. 1-2.

34 John Piper, pp. 22-23.

35 (Matthew 18:19, 21:22; Mark 11:24, John 14:13, 15:7, 15:16, 16:23-24; James 1:5-6, 17; 1 John 3:22, 5:14-15)

But He turned and rebuked them, and said, "You do not know what manner of spirit you are of. For the Son of Man did not come to destroy men's lives but to save them." And they went to another village.

—Luke 9:54-56

So, not only was Jesus' answer "no" to the "calling down fire request," He then took them somewhere else! What's going on here? Which is it, Jesus?

The explanation is quite simple. Asking, "in His name" is a very particular choice of words. To ask "in the name of" a ruling King in those days meant not only invoking the King's authority, but also that the request being made was in accordance with the King's wishes.

To ask "in the name of" required knowing the King's will, and *only* asking (or demanding) that a certain thing be done "in the name of" the King when one was *certain* of the King's will in the situation.

Therefore, thinking you can ask for *anything* and get it is bound to meet with disappointment sooner or later. That's precisely the thinking that renders us "far too easily pleased."

Instead, what if Psalm 37:4 is an invitation to delight in, desire, long for, yearn for, thirst after, hunger for the living, eternal, almighty, all-loving God in whom are hidden all the treasures of wisdom, knowledge, love, joy, peace, etc. And that when we desire God in this childlike manner, He will give us what we've desired—Himself!

Now, that's true, infinite wealth. There is no version of prosperity that can top that! "Whom have I in heaven but You? And there is none upon earth that I desire besides You." (Psalm 73:25) And, "You will show me the path of life; in Your presence is fullness of joy; at Your right hand are pleasures forevermore." (Psalm 16:11)

A Pharisee, an expert in the Law, tried to trip Jesus up by asking Him a similar question. The way he put it was, "Teacher, which is the great commandment in the law?" To which Jesus answered him:

> *"You shall love the Lord your God with all your heart, with all your soul, and with all your mind.' This is the first and great commandment. And the second is like it: 'You shall love your neighbor as yourself.' On these two commandments hang all the Law and the Prophets."*
> **—Matthew 22:37-40**

You see, if we delight ourselves in the Lord; if we love the Lord above all else, then everything else falls into place. Life has meaning. But not *just any* meaning. Our money, wealth, prosperity, ambitions, business, and everything else in our lives takes on a very high and lofty purpose. We get to use all that God has entrusted us with to love and glorify Him and to love and bless people!

Money Won't Make You Rich

As we've seen from the discussion above, money won't make us rich. But this fact implies that we've been handed a weighty responsibility and trust and that involves our money. Jesus put it like this, "Therefore if you have not been faithful in the unrighteous mammon, who will commit to your trust the true *riches?*" (Luke 16:11)

To those who lived a dishonest life before coming to Christ, Paul writes, "Let him who stole steal no longer, but rather let him labor, working with his hands what is good, that he may have something to give him who has need." (Ephesians 4:28) And to those who know Christ and are wealthy, Paul urges, "Let them do good, that they be rich in good works, ready to give, willing to share." (1 Timothy 6:18)

I love that! Let the wealthy "be rich in good works!" When we're rich toward others in our love and generosity, we are "storing up treasures" for ourselves in heaven (1 Timothy 6:19). Much like Jesus' promise to the rich young ruler, when we are generous toward others with what God has entrusted us, we're investing in our future.

Does this work in real life? Celebrity fitness entrepreneur Chalene Johnson, financially successful by anyone's standards, says it's not money that make her prosperous.

"I'm rich in faith," Chalene says, "and Jesus Christ is what makes me rich, not the money. The money is useful because it gives me freedom of choice, and it allows me to better care for people."

This distinction, that Jesus is what makes us rich, means that we store our value in him, not in our money. This is important because we must never derive our value in things that can be taken away from us (like money).

We can be wealthy by this world's standards and yet be poor towards God (Luke 12:21). Since there is no dollar amount or net worth figure that defines the dividing line between wealth and poverty, how can we know if we are prosperous? The behavior which demonstrates our wealth is our generosity towards others.

Should We Give Till It Hurts?

Perhaps you've heard the phrase, "Give until it hurts." This may sound pious, but it's not biblical. In fact, God doesn't want us to give grudgingly or under compulsion. Instead, God loves a cheerful giver! (2 Corinthians 9:7) We are to give as we "purpose in our hearts."

Perhaps a better way to phrase this concept is to "give until it feels good." "Give until it feels right." "Give as you feel the Lord directing you."

When I say the behavior that demonstrates our wealth is our generosity towards others, I mean cheerful, spontaneous generosity. I do not mean a guilt-driven, rule-enforced pseudo-generosity.

We can only experience this kind of generosity when we trust God as our provider. That mindset makes us free from fear, greed, and poverty—because we trust in the flow of abundance.

In a recent conversation, Chalene Johnson told me, "I've never ever worried or approached anything from a scarcity mindset. God will take care of everything, He always does. His track record so far has been 100%. I just always approach everything from that mindset."

A few other observations about giving. First, I believe there are times when the Lord may ask us to withhold a financial gift from someone. For instance, a son or daughter, other relative, a friend, or acquaintance may be in need financially. But it's clear that they've gotten themselves in this situation, as they have many times before. Such a situation requires wisdom from God.

On the one hand, God is very merciful and forgiving. There but by the grace of God go I. On the other hand, God may be using their immediate need as a lever in their life to pry them out of their current lifestyle. If that's the case, we don't want to remove God's lever from their lives.

Second, you and I can't give to everything. Once you get a reputation for generosity (and wealth), people come out of the woodwork asking for money. Again, this calls for wisdom from God. If we're married, we need to be generally in agreement about who and what to give to and how much.

Third, the Scripture is clear that if we have a family member who is genuinely in need, meeting their need should be a priority for us. Paul tells us, "If anyone does not provide for his own, and especially for those of his household, he has denied the faith and is worse than an unbeliever." (1 Timothy 5:8)

Fourth, generally speaking, God does not ask us to give away everything. Remember, Jesus' request of the rich young ruler was a test.

Zacchaeus did not give away everything and Jesus still commended him for his generosity. If we gave away everything, we'd be the one in need and unable to help others!

Fifth, being generous with our wealth does not mean that we don't save for the future. The Bible calls one "wise" who saves up for the future rather than consuming all (or even giving it all away) (Proverbs 6:6; 21:20). Yet, God also warns us about hoarding wealth and putting our trust in it (Luke 12:16-21; 1 Timothy 6:17).

Poverty Won't Make You Righteous

Perhaps the notion that poverty makes one righteous rose from a misunderstanding of the account of the rich young ruler. But as we've already seen, when Jesus told him to give away his fortune, He was testing the man to see where his affections lay. And the man chose his worldly goods over eternal life in relationship with the Lord.

Be assured, the poor can struggle with envy, jealousy, misplaced trust, preoccupation with money, etc. just as much as those who are wealthy. It's just as easy for a poor person to love money as it is for a rich person to do so.

Gnostic philosophy may also have given rise to the idea that poverty makes one righteous. But again, it comes down to a heart issue. Jesus said, "For where your treasure is, there your heart will be also." (Matthew 6:21) As bizarre as it seems, if someone takes pride in their poverty trusting their lack as a means of piety and holiness, then they're actually "treasuring" their impoverished condition. In such a deluded frame of mind, they'll no doubt do whatever it takes to remain poor, banking on the hope that through their poverty they'll win favor with God.

But that's not how God works. Poverty is no guarantee of righteousness.

The Twin Barriers to Joy

Along these lines there are two twin barriers to experiencing joy in whatever circumstances we find ourselves:

1. Unworthiness ("I'm not good enough.")
2. Ingratitude ("God's not good enough.")

Before we come to Christ, there is a sense in which we must see ourselves as "unworthy." In and of ourselves, we are undeserving of eternal life and the inheritance God has prepared for His children. I believe this is what Jesus meant when He said, "Blessed are the poor in spirit, for theirs is the kingdom of heaven." (Matthew 5:3)

But in our state of brokenness and humility, we come to Christ seeking His forgiveness. He does not turn us away, but graciously and mercifully receives us. He not only forgives us but reconciles us with the Father, making us His children. "For you know the grace of our Lord Jesus Christ, that though He was rich, yet for your sakes He became poor, that you through His poverty might become rich." (2 Corinthians 8:9)

Now that we are His children, we must no longer see ourselves as unworthy. Christ has *made* us worthy. "Let us therefore come boldly to the throne of grace, that we may obtain mercy and find grace to help in time of need." (Hebrews 4:16) And, "If you then, being evil, know how to give good gifts to your children, how much more will your Father who is in heaven give good things to those who ask Him!" (Matthew 7:11)

In Christ, we are worthy and have complete confidence in Him! "Now may the God of hope fill you with all joy and peace in believing, that you may abound in hope by the power of the Holy Spirit." (Romans 15:13) In Christ, we have every reason to live in joy!

The other barrier to joy is ingratitude. What ingratitude boils down to is the belief that God isn't good enough. It's the belief that "I deserve better!" This is an insidious state of mind. This was the attitude of many of the Children of Israel as they wandered in the wilderness for 40 years.

God warns us not to *complain* like many of the Israelites did (1 Corinthians 10:10). Complaining, grumbling, dissatisfaction, and discontent all reveal an unbelieving heart. Those emotions expose what we really believe about God: that He doesn't love us or care about us; that He's not good; or that He's not able to give us what we think we should have.

There is no joy in such thinking. It saps us of all that is healthy and good. We demean and belittle God and thereby consign ourselves to a miserable existence.

This is why it's so important that we trust the Lord in all things. Acknowledge His greatness, His goodness, His love always and in all situations. "Enter into His gates with thanksgiving, and into His courts with praise. Be thankful to Him, and bless His name. For the Lord is good; His mercy is everlasting, and His truth endures to all generations." (Psalm 100:4-5)

Live in the knowledge that in His presence is fullness of joy; at His right hand are pleasures forevermore (Psalm 16:11).

Chapter 9

You Don't Have to Give It Away, But You Do Have to Give It Up

• • • • • • • • ● • • • • • • • •

"The reality is that God needs money makers in His kingdom who will be faithful and responsible with the wealth He allows them to create. They are the ones who realize that stewardship is not really so much about what you give but what you allow yourself to keep."
—Milt Kuyers

T he point is not to make money to give it away. When money is alive, active, and circulating, it blesses everyone involved. Business is good in and of itself. But the moment you become attached to the money, or begin to draw your sense of security from it, you are enslaved. The quality of your life is not determined by your bank balance.

Crown Financial, a Christian finance curriculum, encourages its participants to do something symbolic and powerful during their course. It's called a "Quit-Claim Deed."[36] The Quit-Claim Deed looks like a formal document. Its purpose is to acknowledge that God is the owner

---

36 Howard Dayton, *Your Money Counts* (Wheaton, IL: Tyndale House Publishers, Inc., 1996), pp. 24-25.

of all their assets. Properly understood, this is not a decision—for God *does* own everything. Instead, it's simply a formal acknowledgement of that fact.

The point of that exercise is to help us recognize that we are God's stewards of all He has entrusted us with. We are managers, not owners.

> *"I have held many things in my hands and I have lost them all; but whatever I have placed in God's hands, that I still possess."*
> —**Martin Luther**

The Myth of the Starving Artist and Poverty as Virtue

In his book, *Real Artists Don't Starve*, Jeff Goins challenges the myth of the "starving artist." The picture that those two words conjure up for most people is one of the virtuous genius, laboring heroically in obscurity, unrecognized by a world too ignorant to appreciate the artist's work.

This imagery is so strongly ingrained in our thinking that we readily adapt the starving artist mythos not only to painters, writers, and musicians, but to any profession or endeavor. Thus, the CPA, physicist, or entrepreneur is often portrayed as a "starving artist.

The message is clear: within their poverty and their unjust obscurity there is a moral victory. In this way, we unwittingly enshrine poverty as a virtue.

Goins opens his book with the story of Professor Rab Hatfield of Syracuse University in Florence. Hatfield was working to match the dates of the scenes of the Sistine Chapel to the dates when Michelangelo had actually painted each of them.

It occurred to Hatfield that Michelangelo had been paid installments for the work, he might be able to find a paper trail that would help date the paintings. Rab located detailed banking records and began working through the dates. But he soon realized something startling.

He told Goins, "I don't know how much you know about Michelangelo, but usually they taught us that he kind of struggled…"

Michelangelo perpetuated this story himself, often complaining about money. He once wrote that his art had left him "poor, old, and working as a servant of others."

The shocking discovery Professor Rab made? Michelangelo was far from poor. He was quite rich. Rab went on to dig through all the Great Master's banks records, and uncovered a fortune worth approximately $47 million in today's dollars.

While he found this interesting, Rab says he didn't find it very meaningful.

Goins has a different take.

"I disagree," he says. "I think this changes everything."[37]

How? Goins explains that the romanticized vision of poverty as a sign of virtuous creativity is enormously damaging. It is "a useless myth that holds you back more than it helps you produce your best work."

And he doesn't think this is limited to those we traditionally think of as artists.

"We all have creative gifts to share," Goins says. "We are all artists."

This is about more than the expression of our personal creativity (although that is important).

"The world needs your work— whether that's an idea for a book, a vision of a startup, or a dream for your neighborhood—and you shouldn't have to struggle to create it. What does it mean to be a 'real artist'? It means you are spending your time doing the things that matter most to you."

Here's the point Goins is driving toward, and at which *this* book is aimed:

"It means you don't need someone else's permission to create."

---

37 *Real Artists Don't Starve*, Jeff Goins.

Enjoy Your Wealth

It's not only okay to create wealth, it's okay to enjoy your wealth. There are great biblical examples of the wealthy who enjoyed the fruit of their labor: people like Abraham, Isaac, Jacob, Joseph, Job, David, Solomon, Joseph of Arimathea, and Lydia. And Paul instructed Timothy, "Command those who are rich in this present age not to be haughty, nor to trust in uncertain riches but in the living God, who gives us richly all things to enjoy." (1 Timothy 6:17)

We must cultivate a proper, biblical view of our heavenly Father. He does provide for us lovingly and abundantly. If you have children, you know the joy that you experience when you give gifts to your children. Our hearts are full when we watch our children enjoy what we provide for them. So, should we expect any less of our heavenly Father?

If you then, being evil, know how to give good gifts to your children, how much more will your Father who is in heaven give good things to those who ask Him!
—Matthew 7:11

God graciously and benevolently provides us with all things to enjoy.

However, the parable of the rich fool in Luke 12 or that of the rich man and Lazarus in Luke 16 clearly shows that God is not pleased with us when we view our prosperity purely as something to squander.

There is no biblical precedent for self-indulgence. That has nothing to do with God's kingdom. God nowhere encourages His people to "eat and drink and take it easy now that you have reached your golden years." In fact, Jesus spoke harshly about the wealthy businessperson who embraced that lifestyle.
—Milt Kuyers

Anyone who has tried to fill their lives through lazy living knows that those pleasures are fleeting. They only last a short time before one is bored, dissatisfied and left feeling empty. However, real enjoyment of one's prosperity comes with being productive, serving and loving others through (among other ways) the work of our hands and mind.

Rob Tribken, president of BestFresh Foods, has discovered that as a Christian entrepreneur, his business and his mission are one and the same. He explains, "While it may not sound terribly spiritual, I don't like to talk about my *obligation* to help the poor. I just think it's a lot of fun! Our job is to help them succeed."[38]

As a result of Tribken's involvement in Uganda, within four years about 1,200 micro- and small businesses have been launched. Instead of merely giving the poor a handout, businesspeople like Tribken are helping people pull themselves out of poverty through business. In the process, many are coming to Christ. Individuals, families and whole communities are impacted. Now, that's what I call *pure enjoyment!*

---

38 Doug Seebeck, p. 87.

Chapter 10

How to Love People through Prosperity

• • • • • • • • ● • • • • • • • •

"Be a new breed of missionary that demonstrates the gospel by starting businesses that create jobs for the poor."
—**Ernso Jean-Louis**, Haitian Businessman

Traditionally, when we think of helping the poor our minds typically go to: soup kitchens, food pantries, thrift stores and the like. We tend to give the poor a handout. And clearly there are situations that warrant this type of approach for meeting an immediate need.

Indeed, Jesus commends such acts of compassion:

'Come, you blessed of My Father, inherit the kingdom prepared for you from the foundation of the world: for I was hungry and you gave Me food; I was thirsty and you gave Me drink; I was a stranger and you took Me in; I was naked and you clothed Me; I was sick and you visited Me; I was in prison and you came to Me.'
—**Matthew 25:34-36**

However, while such acts show Christ's compassion to the world, I don't believe He intended this as a strategy or remedy for ending poverty. We all get the concept: "Give a man a fish; feed him for a day. Teach him how to fish; feed him for a lifetime."

Successful businesspeople have unique skills, abilities, and resources they can leverage to help eradicate poverty. They can do this in many ways. Below are just a few of those.

Help Change Destructive Mindsets

*"God wants to bless the world He made. Through His death and resurrection, Jesus Christ triumphed over **all** the works of the enemy, including poverty."*
—Doug Seebeck

Generational "attitudes of failure, victimization, inferiority, and inadequacy" often keep the poor, poor. A director of the Land Bank in Nicaragua, Zayda Reyes, explains:

These bondages control the way the farmers think. They restrict them preventing them from believing they can actually succeed. This attitude inhibits an entrepreneurial spirit, blocking them from moving ahead aggressively. What they need most is to learn to destroy these strongholds that are holding them captive to defeat, to failure, to poverty.[39]

The successful businessperson can help reverse these destructive attitudes by coming alongside the individual entrenched in them. A businessperson can share their own story, offer coaching, advice, encouragement, and show them what's possible. Personal relationships

---

39   Doug Seebeck, p. 72.

with people they know, like and trust are the best ways to help these people overcome their flawed ideas.

> *"When the poor understand that God did not plan poverty, does not intend for them to be poor, and wants fullness of life for them, deep changes begin to happen."*
> **—Doug Seebeck**

Another exciting thing happens when one of their own—someone from their own culture, village, or family launches out and starts a viable business—others in that community begin to catch the vision for what's possible!

But we don't have to look abroad to the developing countries to find these self-destructive mindsets. They are very much alive and doing their evil work right here in America—even next door. God may not be calling you to coach someone in another country, but what about the poor here? What about the man or woman you already know who feels beaten down and discouraged?

This is one of the reasons I've chosen to shift the focus of my business to that of helping others succeed.

Provide Business and Technical Expertise

Whether at home or abroad, the successful business person has much to offer in the way of business and technical expertise. Friends of mine like Dan Miller, Cliff Ravenscraft, Donald Miller, and Michael Hyatt have helped thousands launch and sustain successful businesses. In fact, I focus on this mission in my own business. I find it extremely gratifying to know that I'm helping others succeed.

Successful business people who are surrendered to Jesus Christ understand that "successful businesses and business leaders are essential engines to ending poverty."[40] By establishing relationships with new or potential business owners, business people share their expertise and invest in the lives of others—not just financially, but for eternity.

Christ's mission was to set the captives free and He calls us to do the same. As business people, we come alongside the poor to help break poor mindsets and strongholds, give them hope, and show them the way.

In the process of helping others out of poverty, we never want to minimize or neglect the power of the gospel of Jesus Christ to transform lives. But we can hardly just share the gospel with the poor and send them away saying, "Be warmed and filled." Helping them to emerge out of poverty is a great way to grab their attention and to demonstrate the power of the gospel.

Share Your Personal Faith in Christ

Your job is your pulpit and the marketplace is your parish.
—Ed Silvoso

As I've tried to communicate throughout this book, we don't separate our faith in Christ from our business. He wants to be involved intimately in everything we do. How we conduct our business has everything to do with our character and being a disciple of Jesus. Our clients, business associates and business partners we seek to help need to see this inseparable link lived out in our business.

A few years ago, I made a conscious decision to do this and it has radically transformed my business, those I work with, my clients, and me.

---

40 Doug Seebeck, p. 26.

"When you're a follower of Jesus Christ, the more you surrender, the more deeply you will be changed. And the more you are transformed by God's powerful love, the greater is your desire to give your life away to serve others. As that happens, the journey becomes ever more exciting."

—Doug Seebeck

Use Your Wealth to Jump-Start a Business

Another great way successful business people can help wipe out poverty is by loaning money to small business owners in the form of microloans. Notice I said, "loan" not "give." Whether through welfare and other gratis programs in this country or decades of NGO handouts in developing countries, we have inadvertently fostered a sense of entitlement and a spirit of passivity in the recipients.

Free handouts have never been, nor will ever be the answer to eliminating poverty. Only business can do that. Business demands courage, endurance, hard work, and investment. These are all positive values that build people's character and the character of a nation.

But once again, we must strike a balance. Yes, we loan the poor money, but we only charge nominal interest. Our intent is not to get rich on the poor, but to teach business owners responsibility and make such loans sustainable.

One unique way I've found to apply this principle (as have others of my associates) is to offer my courses and programs to my clients at a reasonable fee, but I sweeten these programs with lots of real, tangible, free benefits. In this way, I get to invest in my clients giving them far more than they paid for.

Other Important Ways to Help

Of course, there are many other ways that business people can help eradicate poverty. This can even involve seeking to change current laws or governmental policies. A friend of mine who is a successful businessman moved to a different state about 15 years ago and found their laws extremely archaic and unfriendly toward business. He was able to put five new bills before the state legislature that all passed, making the economic climate much more favorable to business.

Another powerful way we can assist others in business is through our relationship capital. We all know business people who can help a new business owner in some way in which we do not have expertise. I love connecting people! We can achieve some amazing synergy to accomplish great things when we connect people with each other.

Part III

STEWARDING WEALTH: THE PRACTICE OF PROSPERITY

A truly "fruitful" entrepreneur not only starts his own business, he multiplies his effectiveness by helping others do so.
—**Timothy Stoner**

Knowing the truth about prosperity is useless, unless put into action. We sometimes ask questions such as: "How can God allow such suffering in the world?" "Why are there so many who are hungry, poor, sick, and neglected?" "How can God allow this to happen?" The real question is: "How can you and I allow these things to happen?" God has left us in charge of this world, and our job is to bring the reality of His Kingdom into the experience of the people around us. (This is why Jesus taught his disciples to pray for God's will to be done "on earth, as it is in heaven.")

By creating entrepreneurial businesses, and raising up new entrepreneurs, investors, and business people, we do more to eliminate poverty, inequity, and neglect than mere charitable giving will ever be able to accomplish. We empower people to become who God created them to be. The practice of prosperity dictates the degree to which we fulfill our destiny.

Chapter 11

God's Agenda for Your Money

••••••••●••••••••

*We no longer ask, "Lord, what do You want me to do with **my** money?" The question is restated, "Lord, what do You want me to do with **Your** money?" When we have this perspective, spending and saving decisions are equally as spiritual as giving decisions.*

—Howard Dayton

God has a plan for your money: to make you a better person, to make you more like Him, to allow you to participate in banishing poverty, and to bless you. That's right, one of God's agendas is for you to enjoy your life.

In the Bible, I find at least nine principles to live by for stewarding our finances well.

1. **Keep your affections on Christ.** "Lay up for yourselves treasures in heaven, where neither moth nor rust destroys and where thieves do not break in and steal. For where your treasure is, there your heart will be also." (Matthew 6:20-21)

Let Christ be your "pearl of great price." Let Him be your "treasure hidden in a field" for which you sell all else to acquire (Matthew 13:44-46).

2. **Pray for and expect prosperity.** A number of years ago, Bruce Wilkinson popularized the Prayer of Jabez from 1 Chronicles 4:10:

> *And Jabez called on the God of Israel saying, "Oh, that You would bless me indeed, and enlarge my territory, that Your hand would be with me, and that You would keep me from evil, that I may not cause pain!" So God granted him what he requested.*

Though not at all Wilkinson's intent, many saw this verse as a sort of "Aladdin's Lamp," or a secret formula to get whatever they wanted from God. But that is not the intent of this verse. I believe that God delights in answering this prayer for His children. But as we've seen, the primary purpose of prosperity is not necessarily so we can live a luxurious, trouble-free life. We need to check our motives as we pray this prayer and use our prosperity to express love to others and glorify God.

3. **Acknowledge that all you have belongs to God.** When we recognize that what we have God has given to us to hold in trust, it profoundly changes the way we view and handle our money.

4. **Be content, thankful and enjoy what you have.** "Godliness with contentment is great gain." (1 Timothy 6:6) God is pleased when we are content, thankful and enjoy what He has given us. Our contentment and gratefulness demonstrate our trust in Him. We thereby make much of Him.

5. **Save, invest, live simply, and don't consume all you make.** To "live simply" doesn't mean you must live an austere life—it

means you make deliberate choices regarding your lifestyle. You certainly don't make choices based on the opinions of others. In 1899, William Jordan wrote, "Simplicity is restful contempt for the non-essentials of life. It is restless hunger for the non-essentials that is the secret of most of the discontent of the world."[41] Remember, mindless consumption is the enemy of prosperity.

6. **Tithe and give cheerfully and generously.** Jesus said, "It is more blessed to give than to receive." (Acts 20:35) Avoid speculations about whether tithing is for the New Testament age. In Matthew 23:23, Jesus affirmed tithing for New Testament times. Consider giving to be a privilege and part of your stewardship of what God has blessed you with. Giving is an investment. Giving honors God.

7. **Leverage your funds for Kingdom purposes.** Look for ways to further God's Kingdom with your money. What could you do in your business and with your money that would have eternal value? People are really the only thing on earth that is eternal. So invest in people! (HINT: how you pay your employees and vendors could be part of your "ministry.")

8. **Hold your money loosely.** "If riches increase, do not set your heart on them." (Psalm 62:10) And, "For we brought nothing into this world, and it is certain we can carry nothing out." (1 Timothy 6:7) Remember that money is just a tool. It doesn't define who you are and you can't take it with you when you die.

9. **Don't worry about money.** "Therefore do not worry, saying, 'What shall we eat?' or 'What shall we drink?' or 'What shall we wear?' For after all these things the Gentiles seek. For your heavenly Father knows that you need all these things." (Matthew

---

41 William George Jordan, *The Kingship of Self-Control* (New York, NY: Fleming H. Revell, Co., 1899), p. 38.

6:31-32) Instead, trust God implicitly with all your financial needs and dealings.

10. Do you want to be "safe for success"? Then follow what God says about money, riches and wealth. Surrender the false notion that you are somehow different, above all the temptations of riches. Submit to God's way and be safe for success.

Chapter 12

God: Your Wealth Consultant

••••••••●•••••••

"Business is not just business; in reality it is an outstanding Christian calling."
—Timothy Stoner

G od is available to give you the advice, answers, plans, and encouragement you need to run your business and your life. This chapter shows how to invite God into your business, and partner with Him in the marketplace. Learn how to hear from God on specific decisions you face in your business, and your life.

Sometimes we think God is only interested in "spiritual things" and that He has no interest in the material world, and therefore neither should we. This is not a Judeo-Christian idea. It is an idea that sprouts from Greek thinking, and specifically is at the root of a heresy known as Gnosticism, which we've already discussed.

Or we might think that our business issues are beneath the scope of God's concern. But this is false thinking too. Our heavenly Father loves it when we include Him in all facets of our lives. He's interested in all the details. He wants us to trust Him in all things. He offers us wisdom for any and every circumstance:

> *If any of you lacks wisdom, let him ask God, who gives generously to all without reproach, and it will be given him.*
> **—James 1:5**

The truth is from the beginning God wanted to partner with human beings to accomplish His purposes. This is why He put Adam and Eve in charge of the garden. God gave them an assignment, and this was before the fall. That means that work, and the material world, are not evil. They are not results of the fall. What's my point?

When God created the world, He looked at His creation and said it was very good. We should follow His example and enjoy the fact that we can have fun while working. We can rejoice that we are interested in what we do, and celebrate the fact that God made us the way He did. This supports the fact that God enjoys it when we enjoy what He has given us. Thus, God is interested in every aspect of our lives. He longs to give input, supply answers, and help us out. Just as we do for our children.

Another thing we're prone to do is compartmentalize our life. We assume that God wants to be in some areas (church and, family), but not in other areas like business and recreation. But if you separate God from any part of your life, you are not fully trusting or experiencing God. And without Him in that part of your life, you can't fully experience that part of your life either. Business is no exception.

These days, if I am asked if I personally have a consultant for my business, my answer is, "Yes. I have the very best consultant available: God."

Now, most people probably assume that I mean I run my business according to godly principles; principles that I find in Scripture, or that

I am taught by pastors and teachers. While I do this to the best of my ability and as God enables me, this is not really what I mean. Or rather, it is not *all* that I mean.

I mean that I consult with my Lord every day about my business. I'm in constant dialogue with Him about what things to work on, what to write, even how to solve specific challenges and problems I encounter along the way.

Perhaps you've never thought of involving the Lord like this in your business. Consider the following verse: "In [Christ] are hidden all the treasures of wisdom and knowledge." (Colossians 2:3) Think of that! Christ is the ultimate consultant, your resident expert in any and every field and discipline imaginable. With Christ resident in you, why would you not consult Him on a daily basis for your business (and every other) issues?

5 Principles for Practicing the Presence of God in Your Business

So how do we do this? How do we ask God for answers? How do we ask Him for help? Here are five principles I have found useful:

1. **Know that God is interested, willing, and able.** From Scripture we know that God has even counted the number of hairs on your head. We know that one man came to Jesus with an illness and said Jesus could heal him, "If He was *willing*." Another man came to Jesus and asked for help saying, "If You are *able*." The answer Jesus gave to both was "Yes." He was *willing*, and He was *able*. He healed everyone who came to Him.

2. **Realize that you qualify for God's help.** Jesus stepped into the gap between us and God. He solved the "sin problem" once and for all. So just place your faith in Him, and know that you don't

have to "clean up your act," or "make amends" before He will be willing to help you.

3. **Be intentional about what you are asking.** If you are asking for an answer, be specific in your question. If you are asking for help, be specific in your request. I suggest writing down what you are asking for.

4. **Offer thanks immediately.** In Philippians, we are told to make our requests known to God, with "prayer and thanksgiving." Notice how many times Jesus thanked His Father... *before* a miracle happened. There is a unique opportunity to thank God when you are making your request even *before* you've seen the answer with your eyes. That's living by faith rather than by sight (2 Corinthians 5:7).

5. **Expect and look for the answer.** Whether you have asked God for an idea, a connection with a person, or just a miraculous infusion of money, so you can meet payroll... be looking for the answer. Have hope.

What if God *doesn't* answer? Or what if he says *no?*

First, I think the number of times God says, "No" is much lower than we believe it is. When God says, "No," it may be a timing issue, or He simply sees the whole picture that we do not. But He is *always* faithful and true. It's helpful to remember that God's delays are not necessarily His denials.

There's a humorous, but telling scene in the Jim Carrey movie *Bruce Almighty*. Wielding God's power, but lacking His wisdom and omniscience, Bruce decides to unequivocally say, "Yes" to all prayer requests flooding in. As a result, pandemonium breaks out as a million people all win the same lottery.

Trust in God and His response. If He does say, "No" it's for good reason.

At other times, God seems silent. Remember the incident when Jesus was asleep in the boat while His disciples were freaking out in a storm? When they woke Him, He rebuked them for their lack of faith. While Jesus was still asleep, He may have been silent, but He was still present with His disciples. Know that when God is silent, He is still present with you. Can you trust Him in such times?

Finally, we live in a world where evil *is* present and operative. Bad things happen to good people. Seeking God's counsel and doing everything He says doesn't always mean that all will go as you'd like it to go. Consider Joshua and Caleb. Israel sent twelve spies to scout out the land of Canaan before entering it. Joshua and Caleb were the only two spies who said, "Come on! God is with us! We can do this!" Instead, the naysayers won out and as a result the Lord sentenced the Children of Israel to wander in the wilderness for the next 40 years.

My point is that Joshua and Caleb had to live with the consequences of *other people's choices* and the same thing happens to us sometimes. And for reasons often unknown to us, God in His sovereignty allows it. The question is: how will we respond? Will we still trust Him and follow Him?

However, we must finish the outcome of the story. Because Joshua and Caleb trusted God, He blessed them and they did experience prosperity and success in spite of having to live with the consequences of others' choices. The moral of the story: keep trusting in God; keep doing what you know is right!

Finally, I believe that sometimes we're asking for the wrong thing. At times, we may be desperate for a particular response. Perhaps we can't see past it. In our mind, it's so logical. We're preoccupied with it. Why wouldn't God do this for us? So, when God's answer is delayed, or He is silent, or He says, "No," we become desperate—even angry. I have often discovered that in times like this my request is not what I really need. What I really need is *more of Him*.

I believe that when we pray, something *always* happens—*always!* Maybe we don't see it, maybe we don't see it *yet*, or maybe it comes in a form that we don't recognize. Sometimes it's us that needs changing when we pray. Prayer is as much about listening as it is asking. Are we listening to God, or just running through our list of wants?

A useful question that has helped me navigate these waters is one I learned from Graham Cook. When faced with a difficult situation, and I receive no apparent answer from God, I ask, "Who does God want to be for me in this situation?" This is really getting at the fact that I need more of Him.

I have received some of the deepest answers to my own prayers by asking God that question.

You can ask for God's help, for answers, and even for direct assistance. And He will answer you. Try it.

How to Hear the Voice of God

If you could truly receive guidance from God about your career, for your business, and on matters concerning money -would it make a difference? And I don't mean *only* reading the Bible or a devotional, and getting some good principles for being moral and upright business people. What I mean is *hearing* God's voice guide *you* with *specific* advice about your situation, challenges, and opportunities.

Yes, it is possible! And you bet it makes a difference! But rather than try to convince you with a theological argument, I'd like to propose you simply *try* it, and see for yourself what happens.

5 Steps for Hearing the Voice of God

Here are 5 steps to help you hear the voice of God in work, business, and life:

1. **Invite Him into your business (or any part of your life).**
   It sounds simple, but I think it is often overlooked. God
   has granted us each the inspiring, dizzying, and a somewhat
   terrifying ability to accept or refuse His gifts. If we don't invite
   Him into our whole realm of life, including our business, He's
   not going to force His way in. So we begin with an *invitation*.

   In the book of James, we are promised that if any of us
   lack wisdom, all we have to do is ask God and He will give it.
   That's exactly what you're doing when you invite Him into your
   business. This doesn't have to be anything formal or ceremonial.
   You could start with a quiet moment before your workday
   begins, and pray something simple: "Lord, I invite you into my
   business today. Give me ideas, insights, and awareness to make
   the right decisions and to say the right thing in every situation
   that I face today. Help me to honor You in all I do."

2. **Converse with God often.** If I invite you to a party, and you
   show up but I never talk to you, and I never listen to you, how
   much *communication* takes place? Right. Zero. So it's not enough
   just to invite God into your business. He will be faithful to
   show up, but you need to treat Him like you would an honored
   guest at a dinner party. Pay attention to Him. Listen to what
   He has to say. Ask Him questions. A conversation is a two-way
   street. I believe God desires a *dialogue* with us, not a *monologue*.
   So converse with Him often!

3. **Cooperate with Him.** So, you have *invited* God into your
   business. You are *conversing* with Him, learning to hear His
   voice, and becoming sensitive to what He is saying to you. The
   next step is *cooperating* with Him. Because here's the thing: He
   is going to have opinions about what you should and shouldn't
   do in your business. He is going to have ideas and suggestions

for you. Sometimes they may just "pop into your mind," and you might wonder if they are *your* thoughts or *His?* Learning to discern the difference is part of the *communication* step. But the only way you'll ever *learn* is to try *cooperating* with what God is saying to you.

Sometimes, you may mistake your own voice for His (trust me this does happen.) But over time, as you *cooperate* with the voice of God, you will become more and more familiar with His voice. And it is only through *cooperation* that you can move to the next step—*implementation.*

4. **Implement what God has told you to do.** While I think of cooperation as a form of agreement, a way of saying, "Yes, God, that is a good idea. We should definitely think about doing that." There is a step beyond mere cooperation or agreement: this is the step of *implementation.*

I fully believe that God blesses us far beyond what we deserve, can ask, or even imagine. I believe that He is interested in every detail of our lives. I believe that He swings deals our way, that He gives us ideas that will make our business profitable, and that He influences people to do business with us when it's in the best interest of both parties.

At the same time, working *with* God, and having God *with us* at work, does not mean that we are passive. Bill Johnson has said, "Jesus didn't accomplish everything so that you could accomplish nothing." I think that's right, and I would take it one step further, and say that Jesus accomplished everything so that you could accomplish anything... in His name.

What this means is we have to actually *implement* the ideas, strategies, and tactics God gives to us. If you're a farmer, for instance, God might give you a plan for a new crop rotation schedule that could cause your land to yield better harvests. But if you never get up and plow the fields, plant, tend the crops, and bring in the harvest, you'll never reap the reward. Which brings us to…

5. **Trust Him implicitly.** Once we've implemented what God has told us to do, we tend to turn our attention away from Him and look for the results. We've obeyed God, now we expect success. But obedience to Him demonstrated by our cooperation and implementation doesn't always guarantee success—at least not in the way we expect. God may have a different kind of success in mind for us.

Successful entrepreneur, multi-millionaire, and philanthropist Milt Kuyers explains:

Through adversity the successful businessperson has been taught the importance of not giving up. You still have to continue plowing forward through disappointments and discouragements. But if you have one success in the face of 10 failures, that's more than you would have had had you given up or not even made the attempt. These struggles have served to break them of their independence. Now they can joyfully celebrate what God has done, knowing that it was Him, not them, that caused the success.[42]

And the Apostle Paul put it this way:

Therefore we do not lose heart. Even though our outward man is perishing, yet the inward man is being renewed day by day. For our light affliction, which is but for a moment, is working for us a far more exceeding and eternal weight of glory, while we do not look at the things which are seen, but at the things which are not seen. For

---

42 Doug Seebeck, p. 29.

the things which are seen are temporary, but the things which are not seen are eternal.

—2 Corinthians 4:16-18

So, once you've heard from God and you implement what He has led you to do, don't second-guess your actions should things go differently than hoped. Simply trust Him.

That is how you invite God into your business. That is how you see tangible results and God-given answers to your questions and concerns. I challenge you to simply take the five steps, and then see what God does.

Chapter 13

The True Secret of All Success

• • • • • • • • ● • • • • • • •

Transformation has to be a lifestyle—if it is only helping out the poor domestically or internationally, it is just a tithe or a hobby. We have to take Jesus into every facet of our life—our business, our workplace—every area.

—Jerry Haak, Successful Apple Farmer

There is good success and bad success, and you are called to good success. God will not give you anything that will destroy you. The answer to world poverty, genocide, crime, hunger and disease is the Gospel of Jesus Christ. A seldom-recognized way of spreading that Gospel is through the vehicle of entrepreneurial businesses. This is a revolution. And if you're reading this, you are no doubt a revolutionary leader. We need you. Rise up!

Everywhere I go, I see people being robbed. I see *you* being robbed. There are lies and half-truths that are stealing from you every day. Robbing *you*. You are being robbed of customers, profits, success, fulfillment, and peace of mind.

These lies and half-truths are being taught and promoted both by innocent people who don't know any better, and by some who are simply out to take your money, or even your life. These lies are at the root of the problems many Internet marketers are experiencing right now.

Financial Meltdown

Every day, you can find news of financial meltdown in some sector of the economy, or in some part of the world. You don't have to look far to find news of giant corporations teetering on the edge of ruin and collapse, of financial markets draining life savings accounts and pensions, of entire countries needing "debt forgiveness" to bail them out of national bankruptcy.

The news is replete with stories like the Bernie Madoff scandal, the Lehman Brothers banking fiasco (they filed Chapter 11 bankruptcy on bank debt of $613 billion, $155 billion in bond debt, and assets worth $639 billion).

Then there is the ballooning National Debt of the USA, and the ever–precarious state of the behemoth Social Security Administration.

So... Is Everyone in Trouble?

No, not everyone is experiencing this downturn in business. In fact, some are thriving. Many of my colleagues and clients continue to prosper, despite the sometimes discouraging economic climate. I have been blessed to be among those who are prospering.

Here's a shocking fact: almost without exception, those of us who continue to succeed share a common "x-factor." This "x-factor" is the antidote to the lies I mentioned earlier. It is also effective protection against the thief who seeks to rob you. It is the secret of my success. It can be, and should be, yours as well.

The Only Success Secret You Need

Don't worry. I'm not out to sell you anything. I'm going to *tell* you what this mysterious thing actually is, and I'm not going to charge you for it. I received it freely, and I will give it freely to you. But before I do, let me set the stage…

This is the one thing that will give you access to success in all areas…

- Wealth
- Health
- Relationships
- Business
- School
- Love
- Life

This is the one thing that will free you forever from…

- Poverty
- Debt
- Greed
- Sickness
- Depression
- Anxiety
- Addiction
- Fear

This works without you studying, trying harder, or attempting to improve yourself.

In fact, as amazing as it seems, "working hard," or "trying" actually works *against* this "uncommon key" to success I'm talking about. The key itself is a gift and it is, in fact, already yours. All you have to do is accept it.

Tearing Down the Wall Between Sacred and Secular

I've been told more than once that "business and spirituality don't mix." Or, that they shouldn't be mixed. When I do mix them, it seems to make people very uncomfortable.

And admittedly there have been many abuses. Some business people have flaunted their "spirituality" as bait to lure people to do business with them. But later these so-called religious business people proved to be charlatans who conned and took advantage of others.

So, to be polite, and preserve the peace, I've kept the secret of my own success pretty much to myself. But after taking a long hard look at the condition of the people that I know (and love) in business, and in life in general, I decided that silence was no longer acceptable. I felt that I had no choice other than to share this life-changing key to real success.

Self-Help Doesn't Help

If you have bought more than one self-help product or book... you already know, deep down inside, self-help doesn't work. Oh, some of the ideas, techniques, and programs may provide temporary "Band-Aid" fixes for your problems, but it seems like the problems always come back. It seems like the "fix" is always temporary.

Well, I've got some good news. It doesn't have to be this way. You see, the problem with self-help isn't that you lack discipline, or that you just need to try harder, or any other such nonsense.

The problem is more fundamental. You're looking for success in all the wrong places. And trust me, I know. I did too, for a very long time.

When I Finally Embraced This—It Changed My Life

Once I fully realized the power of this "singular success key," my life did a 180° turnaround. The first thing that happened was my miraculous recovery from clinical depression. "Recovery" is not the right term; "healing" is the term that most accurately describes what happened to me.

Most people don't know that in the early 2000's I suffered from deep, debilitating depression. For a short while, I underwent counseling and even took antidepressants. Both of those things are good, and they were helpful to me.

But what is even better is the power of this "x-factor" I'm talking about today—the power that completely healed me of depression. It freed me from taking pills of any kind and completely changed my outlook on life. It gave me my joy back.

The freedom I gained also empowered me to leave a successful radio career to start my own business. And as a result, it enabled me to quickly become one of the most successful direct response copywriters on the Internet.

Doors were open to me that were not open to others; it seemed as though nothing I touched could go wrong; and people were beating down my door to have me work with them.

I believe the same thing that caused my amazing healing, that provided incredible financial abundance, that enriched my marriage in ways I never expected, that gave me an "extreme life makeover" ... that thing is also freely available to you.

I believe that it can change your life the same way it changed mine. And I believe it is time for me to unveil this life-changing success secret, and share with you openly: Doing so has in fact become my life's work.

A Strong Warning

I'm about to tell you exactly what I'm talking about, in just a moment. But let me warn you ahead of time, there will be strong reactions to what I'm about to say.

- Some simply won't believe it.
- Some will be offended.
- Some will find it hard to swallow because of past hurts or injustices.
- Some will think they've "heard it before" (but I believe you've never heard it quite like this).
- Some will think I'm trying to "sell something," or that I'm working some kind of angle. I assure you that is not so.
- Some will unsubscribe, stop reading my materials, and vilify me in online forums.

So be it. But… I urge you, before you refuse the meal, taste and see for yourself if it's good. I assure you it is absolutely the one meal you cannot afford to miss.

How to Receive Success in Everything You Do

Almost everyone I know is looking for "the key" to success in all areas of their life. But most people, as I've already stated, are looking in the wrong places. They are looking for guidance from the wrong people. They are seeking their fulfillment—their success—from the wrong things.

The real answer to all of your problems in life is simple: if you want success and victory in this life, this is my secret (and can easily be yours, too) …

God's Wisdom Always Leads to Success

I'm here to tell you that whatever you need in life, Jesus Christ, who is God in human flesh, is right beside you and ready to help. He wants you to experience success in every way that is good. Not only in some mysterious "afterlife," but in this world... today!

I know this is probably different than anything you may have heard before, but stick with me...

Wisdom from God Will Prosper You in Every Way

When I say that "wisdom from God" will bring you prosperity, I'm not talking about pretty, poetic sayings that sound wise. I'm talking about experiencing a heightened awareness of the right actions to take in life. I'm talking about supernatural intelligence and wisdom that you can have access to right now, today.

You may not know this. Perhaps you've never been taught this. But God says in Scripture that He wants us to succeed. And if you will simply partner with Him, He will guide you through every challenge you face.

He will give you the wisdom and the intelligence and the understanding to make the right decisions—in business, in relationships, and in life in general. God will, in fact, place His "favor" on your life. What that means is, everything you touch will prosper.

And don't worry, there is nothing you need to do to earn this favor from God. In fact, it is impossible for you to earn it. You can only receive it from Him as a gift.

Hear me clearly: when you choose to follow Jesus, He will give you wisdom and favor in all areas of your life. Does this mean that you will never face any problems? No. Of course not. But read this next section very carefully...

Why Bad Things Happen to Good People

Many religious people and churches have been guilty of misrepresenting the nature and character of God. Perhaps you have been the victim of some of this teaching.

One thing that is commonly taught is that bad things happen to us "for a reason." What they're implying is that *God* brought this calamity upon you. Due to sin in your life, a poor decision, even past sins of your parents or their parents, judgment is now being meted out upon you! Their advice: humble yourself and bear it, you have things you "need to learn."

There is no doubt in my mind that there are things that each of us do need to learn. I also know that none of us are free from sin. The Bible also teaches that we can learn much as we rely on God through hardships. As a result of trials, suffering and hardships we can experience growth in our character.

The Bible also says that God uses hardship in our lives to discipline us:

> *It is for discipline that you endure; God deals with you as with sons; for what son is there whom his father does not discipline? But if you are without discipline, of which all have become partakers, then you are illegitimate children and not sons. Furthermore, we had earthly fathers to discipline us, and we respected them; shall we not much rather be subject to the Father of spirits, and live? For they disciplined us for a short time as seemed best to them, but He disciplines us for our good, so that we may share His holiness. All discipline for the moment seems not to be joyful, but sorrowful; yet to those who have been trained by it, afterwards it yields the peaceful fruit of righteousness.*

Therefore, strengthen the hands that are weak and the knees that are feeble, and make straight paths for your feet, so that the limb which is lame may not be put out of joint, but rather be healed.
—Hebrews 12:7-13 (NASB)

But let's be clear about what this passage (and others like it) says. Anything our heavenly Father allows or introduces into our lives He does so as a loving Father. He is gently correcting, instructing, and training us to "share in His holiness." He wants us to become more like Him.

Sure, there are times when His discipline (this training) seems tough and unpleasant, but it is never evil. So let us be clear, when evil things happen in our lives, those are never from God. We must never impugn the character of God, by ascribing evil to Him.

If you latch onto nothing else that I say, please get this and receive it in the core of your being: *God is good, all the time.* That is the one basic truth of life.

When anything bad happens to us, whether it be sickness, financial problems, emotional trouble, or broken relationships... those bad things do not come from God. They come from the enemy of God... commonly known as Satan. Yep, I'm talking about "the devil."

And while "Satan" may sound like an old-fashioned idea to you, it might come as a surprise to learn that he is a real being. And he really has an agenda to do you harm. You see, the devil of Scripture was never portrayed as a red imp with a pointy tail and a pitchfork. He is, in fact, a powerful being who is filled with pride and who opposes God at every turn.

And because God loves you and wants you to succeed—because God has a great destiny for you—Satan opposes that. Satan hates you, and wants you to fail! His agenda is to "steal, kill and destroy." (John 10:10)

Without veering off into some pretty deep theological waters, let's just boil it down to this: good things come from God. Bad things come from the devil.

God wants to spare us the evils that our enemy has planned for us. And that's why He sent His Son, Jesus Christ, to the earth. Jesus did all the work necessary to "pay the bill" for each and every human being on the face of the earth. To give us a clean slate, pay the price for our sin, and make us righteous in the eyes of God.

But that's not all.

The Bible says that Jesus came to "destroy the works of the devil." The Scripture teaches that we can have protection from the schemes of the enemy, that we can be victorious over the evil that he has planned for us. The more you behold Jesus, and the work He has done for you, the more wisdom and favor you will receive from Him.

And through Jesus, God provides a way for you to receive the benefits of blessing. As you behold Jesus, and learn to sense His presence, and walk in His wisdom, you will experience success and favor in your life.

Wait! Is this the "Prosperity Gospel"?

Some critics of what I am saying here will be quick to label me as a purveyor of the "prosperity gospel." Or, as is sometimes derisively known, the "health and wealth" gospel.

Well, would you prefer a "sickness and poverty" gospel?

I'll be quick to admit that I do believe God wants us to prosper.

Now, I am not advocating for those slick, flashy people on TV who encourage you to send in a "seed donation" (to their "ministry," of course) so that God will then act as a "cosmic vending machine" and multiply that money back to you. I really don't believe that is the kind of prosperity God has in mind for us.

His desire for us isn't simply about amassing piles of money and toys to make ourselves feel better or to seem more important than other people. (That certainly misses the point!)

True, biblical prosperity is about receiving everything that God has in store for us and stewarding it for His glory. And everything He has for us is all good, because He is good.

God Favors Those Who Honor Him

All we have to do is look in the Bible itself to see that God showed special favor to those who honored Him. For instance…

David. Most of us know the story of David and Goliath; the young Israelite who faced the giant Philistine in battle and defeated him with a sling. Now, David knew that he could not defeat Goliath in his own strength. David did not trust his own self-effort to give him success in the battle with Goliath. He relied on the power of God. You too have access to that same power. You can trust God to give you victory over the "giants" that you face in your own life; the circumstances, sickness, and challenges that come against you.

Solomon. When God asked Solomon what he desired most, Solomon answered that he wanted wisdom—an understanding heart. The Hebrew word that was used in the original text of this story is *shama*, which literally means a "hearing heart." In other words, Solomon asked for a heart that could hear God's voice. We can ask for the same thing, and God will give us the gift of His wisdom and truth within ourselves. Doesn't that sound like an advantage in life that you would want?

Joseph. You may or may not remember the story of Joseph from the Old Testament, but he faced some pretty hard times in his life. Joseph was sold into slavery by his own brothers. He served his master well, but was falsely accused of a crime he did not commit and landed in prison. He languished in prison for years, apparently forgotten. But even during those dark times, Joseph kept his focus on the presence of God and God blessed him even there. In the end, he was released and promoted to second-in-command over all of Egypt. Just like Joseph, when you learn to be sensitive to God's presence in everything you do (including business and your day-to-day life), you too will experience success.

Jesus himself. Jesus never faced a situation for which He lacked wisdom. We know from Scripture that even when He was a child He amazed the leaders in the Temple with His knowledge of Scripture and of the power of God. When you simply meditate on the Word (the Bible) you are actually meditating on the person of Jesus, because the Bible teaches us that He is the Word become flesh. This is how, through the finished work that Jesus did on the cross, and through the gift of His grace over your life, you are free to walk in wisdom, victory, and success.

It really is that simple.

You don't have to attend church a certain number of times, or say certain prayers over and over again, or do any "work" to receive these blessings of success and prosperity. Jesus did the work for you, and He gives you the results of His work as a gift.

The True Secret of All Success

Jesus Christ is the reason and the source of every good thing that I have experienced in my life.

He has "saved" my soul and made me "right with God." And…

- He healed me from clinical depression.
- He restored my love for people.
- He gave me back my joy.
- He blessed my marriage, renewing and increasing the joy I already had in my relationship with my wife.

- He has given me material blessings beyond measure, and the freedom to do work that I love without fear of external economic conditions.
- He is the reason for my business success.

While I have often talked about being a follower of Jesus in the past, and done so openly, I have never before revealed the true depth of my belief about exactly what it is Jesus has done for me. And what He wants to do for you. But now, the truth is out.

I want everyone to experience the same joy, the same peace, and the same prosperity that I myself enjoy.

I realize that for some, this may be a bit much to take. Please know that is not my intention or desire to offend you—far from it! It's my intention and desire to see you succeed wildly on a whole new scale. This is the purpose for which I have committed my life.

Chapter 14

How to Live this Prosperous Life

• • • • • • • ● • • • • • • •

R emember the three original premises I started this book with? They were the three startling proposals I made in the first pages:

1. God generously offers you prosperity (this includes and goes beyond money).
2. God has a lofty purpose for this prosperity (and it's not primarily that you give it all away).
3. The practice of prosperity is chiefly a spiritual activity (and thus business and wealth creation are holy pursuits.)

I also revealed in the previous chapter that Jesus Christ is the true secret of all success.

If you're still reading, chances are you have at least cautiously accepted those three premises and the preeminent role Jesus Christ wants to play in your life. At this point you may even be thinking, "Ray, you've sold me on this prosperity idea. But how do I start? What's next?"

The rest of this book attempts to answer that question. Let's get started.

4 Principles for Living a Prosperous Life

As with anything worthwhile or valuable in life, prosperity doesn't "just happen." I believe there are four primary principles or practices that stand out as those that lead to prosperity. I've personally experienced the power of these principles in my own business, but they may not be what you might expect.

Principle #1: Find your ultimate joy and satisfaction in God.

Whether you are a Christian or not, it is a well-known fact that merely pursuing money is a lonely and futile pursuit. Studies of lottery winners demonstrate this fact in the extreme. One can amass great wealth and find themselves impoverished emotionally, in their health and in their relationships. In and of itself, financial wealth is a very disappointing pursuit. We need to strive for something much more grand and lofty!

Two brothers came to Jesus one time. Apparently, their father had died and had left all his money to one of his sons. The disinherited son came to Jesus demanding that He tell his brother to divide the inheritance with him. But Jesus, who can read our innermost thoughts, warned the young man: "Beware, and be on your guard against every form of greed; for not *even* when one has an abundance does his life consist of his possessions." (Luke 12:15 NASB)

Then Jesus told the crowd a parable about a man whose wealth increased greatly. But this man's response was to take his ease, to eat, drink and be merry. Jesus declared the man a fool and then wrapped up the story with this summary: "So is the man who stores up treasure for himself, and is not rich toward God." (Luke 12:21 NASB)

But what does it mean to be "rich toward God"?

To be rich toward God means that we find our ultimate joy and satisfaction in Him. King David learned this principle and practiced it. Throughout the Psalms, David refers to God as "The portion of my inheritance," and "My very great reward." David cries out, "You will show me the path of life; in Your presence *is* fullness of joy, at Your right hand *are* pleasures forevermore." (Psalm 16:11)

In Psalm 73:25, the Psalmist declares to God, "Whom have I in heaven *but You*? And besides You, I desire nothing on earth." That is my heart's desire and prayer. How about you?

C.S. Lewis, in an oft-quoted passage from his book *The Weight of Glory*, had the following to say about this principle. (Let the truth of this passage rock your being!)

> *We are half-hearted creatures, fooling about with drink and sex and ambition when infinite joy is offered us, like an ignorant child who wants to go on making mud pies in a slum because he cannot imagine what is meant by the offer of a holiday at the sea. We are far too easily pleased.*[43]

Infinite joy, satisfaction and prosperity *are* available to us, but not in all those earthly things we so obsessively pursue. Our ultimate joy and satisfaction can only be found in the Person of God Himself. I can't adequately express to you the joy I've experienced in making God my chief delight! This one principle alone has radically altered my life and my business for the better.

I hope you don't view this principle as some sort of "bait-and-switch." As John Piper points out, "The radical implication is that pursuing pleasure in God is our highest calling."[44] Recognizing and

---

43 C.S. Lewis, *The Weight of Glory and Other Addresses* (Grand Rapids, MI: Eerdmans, 1965), pgs. 1-2.

44 John Piper, *The Dangerous Duty of Delight* (Sisters, OR: Multnomah Press, 2001), p. 21.

pursuing God as our chief joy and satisfaction is our ultimate goal as human beings. We can't possibly experience true prosperity apart from relationship with Him. Don't seek wealth, let it come to you as you seek the Wealth Giver.

Principle #2: View your business as a means for glorifying Christ.

Let me be clear from the outset what I *don't* mean by viewing your business as a means for glorifying Christ. I don't mean that we should merely seek ways to ornament our business with Jesus slogans and religious bauble.

Instead, what I'm talking about is actually seeing your business as a vehicle for worshiping God and bringing Christ honor. A few years ago, when I finally realized that God had designed me for business and that I can glorify Him by plying my business, it forever changed my life—and my business.

Invite God into every aspect of your business, work and relationships. As God commissioned Joshua to lead the nation of Israel into the Promised Land, He told him:

> *This Book of the Law shall not depart from your mouth, but you shall meditate in it day and night, that you may observe to do according to all that is written in it. For then you will make your way prosperous, and then you will have good success.*
> **—Joshua 1:8**

"The Book of the Law" was God's Word. God had given it to the Children of Israel as a life manual. In essence, God was saying, "Trust Me. Do what I say and involve Me in every aspect of your life and you will prosper!"

As Wayne Grudem explains, we glorify God as we engage in business, because in such activities we're imitating Him.[45] Of course, there's a right and a wrong way to conduct business. If we're greedy, swindle people, or provide them inferior services we're obviously not imitating God. But when we seek to help people and provide them with valuable products and services, we're showing them what God is like. This glorifies Him *and* honors others.

Colossians 1:18 tells us that Christ is to have preeminence in all things. This includes our businesses. Make Christ preeminent; give Him first place in your business. I can't tell you exactly what that will look like for you. But as you set out to make Christ first in your business, He will give you wisdom and insight to know how to do that.

"And whatever you do in word or deed, *do* all in the name of the Lord Jesus, giving thanks to God the Father through Him." (Colossians 3:17)

And believe me, as you do this you will prosper in ways you never thought possible! View and make your business a vehicle for glorifying Christ.

Principle #3: Serve people as a means for loving them.

In business, especially if we're pursuing the almighty dollar, it's easy to disassociate our clients from their humanness. When we do this we tend to see clients as numbers that translate into dollar signs. We dehumanize them. We degrade them. This makes us ugly in their eyes and certainly doesn't demonstrate any part of Christ's majesty and love for them.

When asked what the greatest commandment was, Jesus responded with not one but two: "Love God, and love others." He sees the two commandments as inseparable. We can't love God without loving others. We can never say, "I'm okay with God, but I can't get along with

---

45 Wayne Grudem, p. 13.

so-and-so." No, if we have a problem with one of God's kids, we have a problem with God.

We find a remarkable incident in John 13 that illustrates what I'm talking about. There, Jesus was with His disciples in the upper room. They were celebrating the Passover Feast on the very night that Jesus would later be betrayed. The Scripture says that Jesus knew He was going to be betrayed that night. He knew who was going to betray Him and that He would be cruelly mocked, beaten and crucified the next day.

Knowing all this, Jesus got up from the meal, laid aside his outer garments and wrapped a towel around his waist. Then, in a demonstration of humble love, He served His disciples—yes, even Judas who would later betray Him—by washing their dirty, smelly feet. But look what Jesus told His disciples when He was finished:

> So when He had washed their feet, taken His garments, and sat down again, He said to them, "Do you know what I have done to you?[13] You call Me Teacher and Lord, and you say well, for so I am.[14] If I then, your Lord and Teacher, have washed your feet, you also ought to wash one another's feet.[15] For I have given you an example, that you should do as I have done to you.[16] Most assuredly, I say to you, a servant is not greater than his master; nor is he who is sent greater than he who sent him.[17] If you know these things, blessed are you if you do them."
> **—John 13:12-17**

In that passage, Jesus gives us one of the secrets, one of the principles of prosperity. We will be *blessed*, we will *prosper* if we do as Jesus did. We are to demonstrate our love for others by serving them.

Think about your business. What service and/or products do you offer? Make it your practice, goal and delight to *serve* your clients. See them as people. Your clients have families. They have worries, troubles, heartaches. They have joys too. And they have needs that you can lovingly fulfill. And the fact that they pay you for those products and services is just icing on the cake!

Make it your MO in business to serve people in such a way that they feel loved, honored and cared for. Over-deliver. Serve people as means for loving them.

Principle #4: Continually ask God to bless you.

Just think, you and I have access to the God of the universe, who created and owns everything. Jesus said, "Ask, and it will be given to you; seek, and you will find; knock, and it will be opened to you." (Matthew 7:7) And yet, odd creatures that we are, many of us go through life like paupers.

James hit the nail on the head when he wrote, "You do not have because you do not ask. You ask and do not receive, because you ask with wrong motives, so that you may spend *it* on your pleasures." (James 4:2-3)

So, either we don't ask at all, or we ask, but with wrong motives. Why don't we ask?

To a great extent we don't ask because "we don't want to bother" God with our petty issues. This thinking has the veneer of humility, but is actually constructed on pride. How do I know this? Check out 1 Peter 5:6-7, "Therefore humble yourselves under the mighty hand of God, that He may exalt you in due time, casting all your care upon Him, for He cares for you."

Peter tells us in that passage that we're to humble ourselves before God. Then, he goes on to give us one sure way of humbling ourselves: by "casting all your care upon Him, for He cares for you."

You see, when we don't take our so-called "petty issues" to the Lord, what we're really saying is that He doesn't care for us.

Jesus put it this way, "If you then, being evil, know how to give good gifts to your children, how much more will your Father who is in heaven give good things to those who ask Him!" (Matthew 7:11) Jesus invites us to ask Him for good things.

Another reason we might not ask God for His help, provision, and wisdom may be that we don't deem ourselves worthy of His gracious gifts. Again, God's response to us has nothing to do with *our* worthiness, but instead with *His* grace and love. He graciously gives because of who He is.

The Apostle Paul wrote, "He who did not spare His own Son, but delivered Him up for us all, how shall He not with Him also freely give us all things?" (Romans 8:32)

Clearly, God invites His children to come to Him for anything, anytime. So, take your business to Him daily. Ask for His wisdom, for in Christ are hidden all the treasures of wisdom and knowledge (Colossians 2:3). Do you need a business coach? Jesus Christ is at your service. He *is* the subject matter expert on any and every topic or issue.

But as James pointed out, sometimes we do ask, but we ask with wrong motives. As counter-intuitive as it seems, if you want wealth, don't pursue it. "But those who want to get rich fall into temptation and a snare and many foolish and harmful desires which plunge men into ruin and destruction." (1 Timothy 6:9 NASB) Don't seek wealth, let it come to you.

This doesn't mean we try to "trick" God into giving us what we really want. Instead, go back to the other three principles. It's not only okay, but I urge you to ask God to bless and prosper you. But ask Him with His character and purposes in mind.

We want to pray like Jabez did in the following passage:

Now Jabez was more honorable than his brothers, and his mother called his name Jabez, saying, "Because I bore him in pain." And Jabez called on the God of Israel saying, "Oh, that You would bless me indeed, and enlarge my territory, that Your hand would be with me, and that You would keep me from evil, that I may not cause pain!" So God granted him what he requested.

—1 Chronicles 4:9-10

Remember:

- Find your ultimate joy and satisfaction in God.
- View your business as a means for glorifying Christ.
- Serve others as a demonstration of your love for them.
- Continually ask God to bless you.

Chapter 15

Pathways to Prosperity

· · · · · · · ●· · · · · · · · ·

I n the previous chapter, I laid the foundation for prosperity with the four principles I presented there. Those four principles should be foundational to your business.

Having established that foundation for prosperity, you now want to build on it by focusing on vision, mission, plans, strategies and goals that apply specifically to your business.

Create a Prosperity Pathway

There is power in a prosperity pathway. A prosperity pathway helps you:

- Develop clarity about how to proceed
- Focus on achievable outcomes
- Stay on course

Begin with Your Vision

A prosperity pathway begins with a vision. Your vision is a concise picture of what you want your business to look like or have accomplished at some future date. You're dreaming about your future state. The vision for my business is to help one million entrepreneurs achieve true prosperity while glorifying God.

In creating your vision, project what you want your future business to look like or achieve. What legacy do you want your business to leave behind? In what ways do you want your business to change the world? Go back to the four principles to help you determine a lofty vision for your business.

Next Step: Your Mission

Mission differs from vision in that it is present- and action-driven. Your mission is what you attend to day-in-and-day-out. My mission is to help people start, run and grow their own business so they can change the world. This is what I do every day. Also, notice how my mission supports my vision. Your mission must focus on your vision. Then, out of your mission you formulate strategic plans.

Strategic Plans

Your strategic plans should encompass plans, strategies and systems that you put in place in order to fulfill your mission. These elements all depend greatly on the type of business you run and your gifting.

For example, in my business I employ the following strategies:

- Podcasts
- Blog articles
- Newsletter

- Website
- Courses (both live and virtual)
- Mastermind groups
- Network with influential people who get things done
- Product-launches
- Speaking engagements
- Joint venture launches with other business partners and affiliates

I then plan my calendar around these strategies. For instance, I record a weekly podcast; I write a monthly newsletter; I determine how many product-launches I want to do in a year; etc. I set goals for myself in each of these strategies and we'll get to goal-setting shortly.

All of these strategies require systems. I can't emphasize enough how important it is to establish systems that govern each of these strategies. You create systems by breaking down a particular strategy into its components. Ask yourself, for example, what are all the elements of creating a podcast each week?

Some of those elements include:

- Brainstorming topics
- Researching and making notes about a topic
- Writing a script outline
- Rehearsing and recording the podcast
- Editing the podcast
- Designing/choosing a graphic to accompany the podcast
- Transcribing the podcast
- Creating shownotes and a transcribed version
- Editing the shownotes
- Publishing the podcast, shownotes and transcription on the web

Each of those elements requires a system in place. Having systems in place ensures consistency of procedure and product. Systems prevent you from forgetting things. Systems help your business run smoothly. I highly recommend Michael Gerber's book, *The E Myth Revisited* to help you with designing systems.

As your business grows, employees or virtual assistants may pick up certain elements of a strategy for you. This is where I am in my business. As a result, I don't have to personally execute all ten of those elements every time I create a podcast. I still have to do some of them, but I currently engage about seven virtual assistants to help me with various elements of creating a weekly podcast. (Each one of these virtual assistants works in the area of their expertise.)

This factor further emphasizes the importance of having systems. Because I engage so many helpers in publishing a podcast, we would have mass chaos without specific systems in place.

When you're just starting out, you personally may have to work all the elements for a given strategy. Because of that, there's a real temptation to just "wing it." But I urge you to begin creating processes and systems from the get-go. That way, you won't have to rethink each step or element as you execute them and you'll get a more consistent product every time. This is the way franchises work and it's one of the main reasons they're so successful. They create a reproduceable model.

Finally, by creating systems and putting them in place now, when you do grow and begin to engage employees or virtual assistants, you'll be that much farther ahead.

Goals

With your vision, mission, strategies and systems in place, you need to set goals to achieve new levels of productivity and prosperity. Perhaps you've heard the acronym SMART Goals. SMART stands for:

S—Specific
M—Measurable
A—Achievable
R—Realistic
T—Time-based

SMART goals are a good place to start. For instance, a SMART goal I set for my business some time ago was to produce a high quality, relevant, success-building podcast each week. Notice that my goal meets the requirements of being "SMART."

But sometimes other goals we set for our business are not so clear-cut. For instance, let's say that I want to set a goal to do one million dollars in revenue this year. The problem with conventional goal-setting in this fashion is that it's:

- All or nothing
- Pie in the sky
- Demoralizing
- Demotivating

In other words, if at the end of the year I don't make my goal, I feel a sense of failure. Even if I did better than I've ever done before, I still didn't hit my goal. Also, where did I pull that million-dollar number from? Was it just a "pie-in-the-sky" guess? Again, not hitting a singular goal like this can be demoralizing and demotivating—two deadly emotions for the entrepreneur!

But the alternative of not setting goals isn't an option either. Goals help us improve our performance, stretch, learn new things, make more money, help more people, etc. Without goals we have no idea how we're doing, or where we're heading.

So, here's what I suggest and what I do: I set BAM! Goals. BAM is also an acronym and stands for:

B—Baseline
A—Amazing
M—Miraculous

With BAM goals we set one goal with all three levels of attainment.

A *baseline* level is realistic, reflects past performance, and you're pretty sure you can hit it, because it's what you routinely do.

An *amazing* level causes you to stretch, requires hard work, and would represent a home run for you.

A *miraculous* level is a goal beyond your current reach. It seems impossible! In fact, it would require a miracle!

I call this BAMifying your goals. For instance, let's say you've got a writing business that you've recently started. You might BAMify your monthly revenue goals like this:

Baseline—$2,500/month
Amazing—$10,000/month
Miraculous—$25,000/month

You don't choose *which* level you'll shoot for. Instead, you put *all three levels* in front of you. What I have discovered is BAM goals are flexible, more achievable, and help you stretch. By including the Amazing and Miraculous levels, you open your mind to what's possible and you start thinking grander and behaving in ways that help you achieve a higher level than you once thought available to you.

Choose Your Own Adventure

In this chapter we've looked at how to create a pathway to prosperity that includes establishing your vision, mission, strategic plans, strategies and goals. In the next chapter, we'll look more closely at a dozen Prosperity Plans to choose from.

Chapter 16

Entrepreneurial Prosperity Plans

• • • • • • • •●• • • • • • • • •

T o begin with, let's recognize that we are in "a new renaissance" for
entrepreneurs.

We have entered an exciting era—the Digital Business Era. While
you have always been free to start, run, and grow your own business, it
has never been easier to do so than now. Most of the barriers to entry
have been removed.

In the past, those barriers were five-fold:

1. **Investment capital.** In the past, the initial investment to start a
    small franchise (like a sub shop) could be $200,000-$500,000.
    While this amount varied widely, it was out of the reach for
    most average persons wishing to start their own business. It was
    still possible to do so, it was just very, very costly and very risky.

2. **Geography.** In the pre-Internet days, and even in the early
    years of the Internet itself, most businesses were still limited by
    their geography. Whether this meant they were limited by the
    area in which they could perform their service, or limited by

the fact they could not deliver their products to certain places economically, their geography limited their potential profits. The internet lowered that barrier as it became possible to deliver many products digitally at virtually no cost, or physically at very low cost.

3. **Technology.** This was, until recent years, a real barrier most people do not think about. But with today's smart devices, and super high-speed connections, we can perform tasks via technology that would've cost hundreds of thousands, if not millions of dollars, in the past. This includes Print-On-Demand services, automated shipping and transaction services, outsourcing, and more. Now we can perform these tasks for pennies, repetitively, in an automated fashion.

4. **Distribution.** In the mail order business of the past, you could sell virtually anything to people all over the world. The problem was distributing it. Many items were prohibitively expensive to ship. When it came to things like books, training programs, seminars and workshops, those were obviously limited by your ability to ship them or perform them. Now trainers, coaches, speakers, teachers, artists, musicians and more can use digital distribution to multiply their reach.

5. **Marketing.** Once the province of monolithic corporations such as Procter & Gamble, digital technology now makes it possible for any business owner, no matter how small their operation, to take advantage of sophisticated marketing techniques such as automated follow-up, testing and tracking of ads, and customer relationship management approaches.

Now each of these "barriers to entry" has been removed or lowered sufficiently for anyone with an idea and an internet connection to play the game.

12 Types of Businesses You Can Start With $100 and Grow to 8 Figures

Here are 12 basic business models that almost anyone can start, most with $100 or less.

1. **The Merchant.** This is a familiar, traditional business model. When we refer to The Merchant, we mean a business owner who buys physical items at wholesale, offers them through physical store location, marks up the price and sells at retail. Think of this as any brick-and-mortar operation, including mail-order businesses that ship physical items through the Postal Service.

2. **The Maker.** The Maker is the person who makes physical objects and sells them for profit: these may be articles of clothing, jewelry, decorations, even electronics and widgets made through technologies like 3-D printing. This is the digital era's version of local hand-craftsmanship.

3. **The Impresario.** This business model is centered upon the person who arranges live events, such as seminars, workshops, and large group trainings. The impresario takes the financial risk of booking the venue, contracting the speakers or teachers, and then marketing to fill the seats. Profits are made on ticket sales, or perhaps on items sold at the event itself. One of the higher risk businesses on this list, but also one of the most potentially profitable.

4. **The Media Creator.** This business model includes anyone who creates digital media for distribution. Podcasters, YouTubers, and others who create media to be distributed online fall into this category. In my opinion, this is one of the areas of highest potential growth in the foreseeable future.

5. **The Media Publisher.** Some people prefer not to create, but rather find the creators who prefer not to market. The people

who gather together creatives and give them a platform from which to sell and distribute their work are Media Publishers. If you see the potential of selling digital media, but don't feel you are creative in that way, this is how you cash in on the media creation phenomena.

6. **The Freelancer.** Freelancing can be and should be a lucrative way to offer one's skills as a service. It is a viable business model, though it is wholly dependent upon the freelancer's ability to provide the service contracted for. In other words, if you don't work, you don't eat. Everything is dependent solely upon you and your personal efforts. In today's Internet-based economy there are ways to mitigate this problem, and still build a reliable business as a freelancer. Just know that the two chief dangers of this business model are (A) relying on only one stream of income and (B) undervaluing and underpricing your services.

7. **The Engineer.** Whenever you hear an entrepreneur say, "I'm not a tech person" or "I wish someone could tell me where I can find a good tech person," you're hearing market potential for the Engineer. The Engineers are the people who know how to set up WordPress, operate plug-ins, integrate with Software as a Service (SaaS) providers, and generally understand the mysteries of this arcane system we call the Internet. This category also includes those genius programmers who create new software and services, and outright Inventors.

8. **The Teacher.** This is one of the most revolutionary categories of business available to virtually anyone today. Each of us possesses some kind of wisdom, experience, and knowledge that is unique to us. These are things that only we can share and teach. And for each of us, there is an audience large enough to support us well for the rest of our lives. Knowing how to monetize your knowledge and experience is a popular topic. Care must be taken

not fall victim to charlatans and "get rich quick" scammers who offer fraudulent schemes. There are many reputable teachers and programs that help you accomplish building this kind of business. Just be careful who you trust.

9. **The Artist.** Artists are one of the greatest beneficiaries of the Internet's geography and distribution-flattening qualities. No longer are you dependent upon a gallery to display your work. You can be your own gallery. No longer are you dependent upon a publishing firm to offer your prints or reproductions for sale. You can offer them yourself. The opportunities for artists in today's digital era are truly astonishing.

10. **The Consultant and/or Coach.** The consultant is a powerful ally for business people and the general populace alike. People engage consultants to help them solve problems or increase efficiency. It is possible to be a consulting expert in virtually any area of specialized knowledge: from dental or medical practice, to finding more efficient ways to distribute products, to creating marketing programs that work, to almost any subject you can name. The Coach is like a consultant, and sometimes the two are confused. The distinction I draw is that the Coach serves not only as of resource of knowledge and techniques, but mainly as an encouragement and accountability partner. Truly great Coaches can elicit performances from their clients that the clients cannot or will not produce on their own.

11. **The Blogger.** Even though this topic is not as "hot" as it once was, we are witnessing a Renaissance in the area of blogging. If you're a writer who wishes to bypass publishers and paper-and-ink altogether, and build an audience online, this is your ticket. There are a dozen ways to monetize a well-read blog. And you do not need a gigantic audience to make it worth your while. 1,000 loyal readers are enough to support you in a six-figure

income as a blogger. And at that level your expenses will be virtually nonexistent.

12. **The Thought Leader.** If you have a truly powerful and Unique Core Thesis ™, substantive ideas that go beyond the typical how-to material and cross over into Wisdom territory, you may wish to become a Thought Leader. In the old days, one had to be anointed as a Thought Leader by the Publishers and Pundits. No more. Now, in the words of Seth Godin, you can "pick yourself." It's possible to anoint *yourself* a Thought Leader. Doing so allows you to extend your business into many of the previously listed models, and may include publishing books, video and audio training programs, live seminars and workshops, consulting, coaching, and more. This is perhaps one of the most lucrative opportunities available to virtually anyone today. Intelligence, competence, confidence, and commitment are required to succeed.

For free assessments, ideas, tools, and training in how to start, run, and grow one or more of these businesses, please visit our website at RayEdwards.com. Our mission is to help entrepreneurs achieve prosperity with purpose. It will be our pleasure to serve you.

Chapter 17

The Doors of Destiny—
Unlocked and Wide Open

• • • • • • • • ● • • • • • • • • •

*I call heaven and earth as witnesses today against you, that I
have set before you life and death, blessing and cursing; therefore
choose life, that both you and your descendants may live; that
you may love the Lord your God, that you may obey His voice,
and that you may cling to Him, for He is your life and the length
of your days.*

—Moses in Deuteronomy 30:19-20

T he choice is now yours. Now that you know the secret to an
abundant life, what will you do? The doors of destiny are wide
open, and you must choose whether to step out and take destiny into
your hands.

I urge you to follow Jesus. Make Him your Confidant, Counselor,
and include Him in all you do.

Become rich beyond your wildest dreams, rich in the way God
means rich—which dwarfs our concept of being rich and reduces our
highest aspirations of wealth to mud pies.

As we have seen, being God-rich means having money and possessions—and health, peace, love, joy, fulfilling work, robust relationships, and abundant joy in every area of our lives.

Imagine What 1,000,000 Kingdom-Oriented Millionaires Could Do

What if this is the time in history when we, the Body of Christ, rise up to demolish the mindsets of both poverty and greed that have a grip on so many? What if we are privileged to be part of the solution?

The goal of my work is simple: to mentor, equip, and lead 1,000,000 people to become millionaires. Not to become millionaires for the reasons the world normally supposes people want to be rich. Not so that they can buy the biggest house, or the fastest sports car, or acquire the "most toys."

Our aim (and my personal mission) is to develop "Kingdom millionaires." People who seek to accumulate wealth to do the work of God's Kingdom; people who build and lead businesses for His glory.

Leading 1,000,000 people to become millionaires means bringing one billion dollars into alignment with God's Kingdom—money that will be used for His purposes.

Over the last few years, I've had the great privilege of working with many well-known business people and thought-leaders. Some of my clients are household names. I've been able to contribute to their success, and my work has been responsible, in part, for bringing millions of dollars into those businesses and those personal fortunes.

Now, I am dedicating my work to the sharing of God's Kingdom. How? By continuing to help people and businesses create more wealth, but now with a renewed and more focused purpose. By being dedicated...

- To the destruction of the poverty-and-greed mindset.
- To the creation of new wealth.

- To the alleviation of suffering, sickness, and poverty.
- To fighting evil and the works of the devil. We are in a world at war. It's Good against evil.

While evil wants to take over, we resist the idea of giving up a single inch of ground.

This is the sound of a revolution.

If You're Receiving this Message, You Are a Revolutionary

If this resonates with you, if you want to be part of this revolution, I invite you to step up.

As dark as some people think tomorrow looks, we have a different view. We believe the future is pregnant with promise, and we are committed to taking back tomorrow from the "gloom-and-doomers."

So how can you join in?

First, and most importantly, make sure you are following Jesus. If you don't already know Him, accept Him as your Lord (your Master) and as your Savior. It's not complex. All that is required:

If you declare with your mouth, "Jesus is Lord," and believe in your heart that God raised him from the dead, you will be saved.
—Romans 10:9

You see, the Bible tells us that we have all sinned and that the wages of sin is death. But the free gift of God is eternal life in Jesus Christ. When we trust Him for forgiveness of our sins, He declares us righteous before God. This is not something we earn, but His gracious gift to us. In gratitude for what Christ has done for us, by dying in our place, we follow Him. In this way, we have a new life, just as Christ rose from the dead.

Build that life, and the wealth that is part of it, upon a foundation of God's Kingdom principles—for Kingdom purposes.

And like John, the beloved disciple of Jesus, I pray that you are in good health and that you prosper in all things, even as your soul prospers.

About the Author

Ray Edwards is a Communications Strategist, Copywriter, and the author of *How to Write Copy That Sells*. His podcast, The Ray Edwards Show, is consistently one of the top-ranked shows in Apple Podcasts and has been downloaded over 1.5 million times. Ray has worked on copy and marketing with some of the most powerful voices in leadership and business. He's helped generate an estimated $400 Million in revenue for clients like Tony Robbins, Michael Hyatt, Dan Miller, Jeff Goins, Jack Canfield, Frank Kern… and many more. He's been featured on Forbes.com, SocialMediaExaminer.com, and Entrepreneur.com. Find out more at RayEdwards.com

CPSIA information can be obtained
at www.ICGtesting.com
Printed in the USA
JSHW021822260121
11240JS00003B/48